Solitude an

A Buddhist View

Sarvananda
(Alastair Jessiman)

indhorse Publications

In describing the experience of being on the far side, in the dark, facing out toward the impenetrable depths of the cosmos and separated from all humanity by the bulk of the Moon – out of sight and unreachable and utterly, utterly alone – Collins actually used the word 'exultation'.

Andrew Smith, *Moondust*, Bloomsbury, London 2006, p.90

Dedication

This book is dedicated to my teacher, Sangharakshita, with continuing gratitude and admiration.

Published by
Windhorse Publications
169 Mill Road
Cambridge
CB1 3AN
United Kingdom

info@windhorsepublications.com
www.windhorsepublications.com

First Edition 2012

Typeset and designed by Ben Cracknell Studios
Cover design by Deborah Harward and Marlene Eltschig
Cover image © Ken Hurst
Printed by Bell & Bain Ltd, Glasgow

British Library Cataloguing in Publication Data:
A catalogue record for this book is available from the British Library

ISBN: 978 1 907314 07 0

About the Author

Sarvananda (Alastair Jessiman) was born and educated in Glasgow. In 1987, after being ordained as a member of the Triratna Buddhist Order, he moved to Norwich where, over the last twenty years, he has taught classes in Buddhism and meditation. He earns a living by writing and has had ten plays and two comedy series broadcast on BBC Radio. Sarvananda is also the education officer for the Norwich Buddhist Centre and has a particular interest in meditation. He is the author of *Meaning in Life*, another title in *A Buddhist View* series.

Acknowledgements

I'd like to thank Jinamitra and Priyananda of Windhorse Publications for their help and encouragement. I'd also like to thank Doug, Elaine, Shona, Robbie, and Roori for allowing me the use of Coll Cottage for solitude and writing.

Contents

1

Introduction

Footprints in the Sand

I am out of humanity's reach,
I must finish my journey alone,
Never hear the sweet music of speech –
I start at the sound of my own.[1]

William Cowper, 'The Solitude
of Alexander Selkirk'

When I was considering the themes of solitude and loneliness for this book, some of the first images that came to mind were from a children's television series that was made in the 1960s: *The Adventures of Robinson Crusoe*. The series was based on the 1719 novel by Daniel Defoe, which told of the resourceful Crusoe, the shipwrecked sailor, who learnt to survive and thrive on an (initially) uninhabited desert island. The television series (which always seemed to be on in the school holidays) came to enthral a particular generation of children who were captivated by the programme's handsome hero, beautiful locations, and lovely, haunting, and melancholy score. A particular sequence from the programme has always remained in my mind, and it's the same sequence that my friends often cite when remembering the series. In this, the hero discovers a set of footprints in the sand, and follows the tracks with growing excitement, believing that they'll mean an end to his isolation. But the tracks lead him in a wide circle, back to the very point where he first discovered them. They are in fact his own footprints and, when Crusoe realizes this, we share his crushing sense of disappointment . . . Why was it this particular episode that remained in my mind, and in the mind of my friends? It was as if, even as children, this sequence of images seemed oddly and uncomfortably familiar to us, touching, as it did, some deep feeling of insecurity in our hearts.

Robinson Crusoe, the original novel, was inspired by the true story of Alexander Selkirk, a brave and obstinate Scottish sailor, who came into conflict with the master of his ship, one Captain Stradling. Selkirk and Stradling were at loggerheads over the seaworthiness of their vessel, the *Cinque Ports*, and the argument ended with Selkirk demanding to be put ashore on the uninhabited island near which they were anchored. Perhaps Selkirk expected to be followed by enough of the near-mutinous crew to prevent the ship from sailing. If this was Selkirk's plan, it didn't work. Nobody joined him and, as the ship pulled away, Selkirk, rather endearingly, panicked, and screamed to be let back on board. But Stradling ignored the Scot's cries and the *Cinque Ports* pulled away, leaving Selkirk staring after the vanishing ship in horror.

Alexander Selkirk remained on the island for four years and, for the first year or so, was constantly assailed by depression and fear. Eventually, however, he came to relish his stay on the island, coming to believe it had made him 'a better Christian' than he'd ever been before – or feared he ever would be again. When he was finally rescued, he received his rescuers with a benign indifference and, in later years, 'bewailed his Return to the world, which could not, he said, with all its enjoyments, restore him to the Tranquillity of his Solitude'.[2] Selkirk would surely have responded with understanding to these lovely verses composed by one of the Buddha's disciples:

Come then! Alone
I will go to the wilderness
praised by the Awakened One
pleasant for a resolute monk
dwelling alone.

Alone,
astute in my goal,
I'll quickly enter the grove
– refreshing,
giving rapture
to meditators –
the haunt
of elephants in rut.

When the Cool Forest's in full flower,
in a cool mountain gorge,
having bathed my limbs,
I'll walk back & forth,
alone.

Ah, when will I dwell,
alone and free from companions,
in the refreshing great forest –
my task done . . .[3]

Some of us are naturally drawn to solitude. For others, the idea
of being on our own, whether in the wilds or even in the privacy
of our room, can seem like a very unattractive option. Loneliness
is an emotion that many of us seek to avoid at all costs and, for
those of us for whom this is true, solitude and loneliness may
appear synonymous. In this book, we'll be looking at the Buddhist
perspective on loneliness and how a Buddhist might deal with

this problematic emotion. We'll also be exploring in what way time spent in solitude can be of benefit on the Buddhist path, and we'll be investigating the seeming paradox that, in facing up to our essential aloneness, we come to recognize how essentially connected to others we truly are.

It's tempting to begin this book in the spirit of the Buddhist verses above, by wading in, and enthusing about the delights and pleasures of solitude. But the truth is that usually, before we can reap the benefits of solitude, we must first face up to our loneliness. So let's begin with loneliness. Let's imagine ourselves in the shoes (or bare feet) of Alexander Selkirk, before he begins to relish his solitary sojourn on his desert island . . . Here we are then, standing knee-deep in the ocean, watching as our ship begins to disappear over the horizon. Above us is a vast, cloudless, blue sky. Before us is an infinite stretch of sea. We listen to the lonely cries of the gulls, the bleating of the wild goats, the sound of the wind in the palms, the waves falling gently on the shore . . . We are utterly, utterly alone.

Coconut anyone?

2

Loneliness

The Theme of Everyone

I fear me this – is Loneliness –
The Maker of the soul
Its Caverns and its Corridors
Illuminate – or seal[4]

Emily Dickinson

Loneliness

In 1925 an Anglo-American film-maker made a silent movie about a gold prospector who struggles for survival in the icy wilderness of the Klondike. The first scene shows a long line of prospectors roped together, inching up a snow-blasted slope. We then cut to the hero of the film as he haphazardly, and entirely on his own, attempts to negotiate a precipitous mountain pass. He does this with a confidence that we, the audience, don't entirely share. Shots of the wild and desolate Alaskan landscape highlight the character's isolation and loneliness.

In the following scenes we see him coping with this loneliness, as well as with blizzards, bears, and hunger. His eyes become ever darker as he begins to look starvation in the face. At one point, a companion almost resorts to cannibalism. Terrible winds howl outside his isolated cabin. The hero is finally forced to take desperate measures. We watch as he opens the stove and removes the roasting tray on which rests his right boot. With a spoon, he bastes the boot with boiling water, as if this liquid is the most delightful gravy. He then serves up his meal with all the precise ritual of somebody serving up a Sunday roast. He sharpens his knives, carves, tastes the leather, considers, and gives a small nod of appreciation. Then he proceeds to pick the nails of the boot as if they were the bones of a delightful capon and rolls the laces round his fork as if they were strands of spaghetti.

Later in the film, in slightly improved circumstances, our hero visits a saloon-cum-dance hall in one of the settlements that has grown up in the wilderness. Here, he's immediately and thoroughly captivated by one of the dancers. At one point the beautiful girl stands right next to Charlie, our hero, who hardly dares breathe. Yet she's totally oblivious to his presence, looking right through him. It's only when she decides to dance with the shabbiest, most unprepossessing man in the hall (in order to spite her lover) that her eyes properly alight on our hero. She asks the tramp to dance and Charlie takes her affectionate attentions as overtures of genuine love.

Later, the girl and some of her friends, for a joke, visit Charlie, flirt with him, and then accept his invitation for New Year's dinner. When New Year arrives we see our hero in a state of high excitement, having prepared his dinner table with candles and name cards and little presents. As he sits at the table, waiting for the girls to arrive, he falls asleep and dreams of the evening to come. We watch him performing an intricate ballet for the girls with two bread rolls on forks, an exquisite little pantomime that the women find utterly delightful. The evening is full of laughter and promise. But, when Charlie wakes up, the candles have burnt down. The girl and her friends have not arrived. Charlie stares out of his cabin door and we can observe, in that tragic stare, his realization that the girls will never come. He wanders over to the town where, in the dance hall, everybody is joyfully bringing in the New Year. Charlie gazes through the window at the party and, on his face, we see an expression of the utmost loneliness and yearning. Once again we witness Charlie as the perennial outsider, looking in upon the world and longing hopelessly for his share of the riches, food, comfort – and love.

The film is Charlie Chaplin's *The Gold Rush* and I was surprised, watching it recently, how funny and moving the film is, how well it holds up eighty-five years after it was made, and how happily I accepted the pathos. *The Gold Rush* was the film for which Chaplin most wanted to be remembered. It combines glorious comedy with memories of the abandonment, deprivation, and hunger that haunted him all his life. Above all, the film most successfully encapsulates one of Charlie Chaplin's major themes – loneliness.

For many years, Charlie Chaplin was the most famous man in the world. His little tramp seemed to embody an everyman figure who, in his silence, could speak to kings and commoners in their own language. Chaplin was mobbed at train stations and airports all over the globe. He was the honoured guest of a host of international celebrities, including the crown prince of Japan, Albert Einstein, Diego Rivera, Pandit Nehru, Pablo Casals, Nikita Khrushchev, Jean Cocteau, and Chou En-lai. One of the reasons for this massive popularity was his ability to portray loneliness, and to lessen the sting of that loneliness with the comedy and pathos of recognition.

A film like *The Gold Rush* helps us recognize a truth: that we are *all* outsiders looking in – whether we be a shabby tramp or the crown prince of Japan. That recognition makes us less lonely, and it invests our loneliness with a certain shared, ragged dignity. For loneliness is a state of mind that can often undermine our sense of dignity and self-confidence.

In his autobiography, Chaplin said:

> Loneliness is repellent. It has a subtle aura of sadness,
> an inadequacy to attract or interest; one feels slightly
> ashamed of it. But, to a more or less degree, it is the
> theme of everyone.[5]

Loneliness is something we can find very difficult to admit to,
even to ourselves. To recognize our own loneliness, to 'confess' it to
a friend, can feel like an admission of failure. 'We should be more
self-sufficient,' we tell ourselves, 'less needy.' We look at the people
around us and notice how self-sufficient they seem, how happily
hitched up, how outgoing and gregarious, how deeply involved
in a club, group, society, community, gang, or clique. How many
friends they have. How popular they are. We compare our own lives
unfavourably. We forget that, as Charlie Chaplin said, to a greater
or lesser degree, loneliness is the theme of everyone.

The realization that my parents were human beings in their
own right and not merely *my parents* dawned on me slowly
during my teens. But there was one particular incident, quite
unremarkable in itself, in which the realization came home to me
quite strongly. After dinner one evening I was about to leave the
house to see a friend. My mother and brother had already gone
out on missions of their own. In the hallway my father, hands
in pockets, gave me a rather sad smile and told me to enjoy my
evening. And as I closed the door, I knew, with a kind of poignant
shock of recognition, that my father, at that moment, had felt
lonely. It was perhaps my first moment of real empathy.

Various friends have told me that loneliness is an emotion
they very rarely experience, and I've no reason to disbelieve them.
So, if it is indeed the theme of everyone, loneliness must mean
more than just the conscious, painful experience of being home
alone on a Saturday night. The truth is that we very skilfully,
and often unconsciously, organize our lives in such a way as
to avoid loneliness. It is the fear of isolation, of being lonely, of

being rejected by the group or the person on whom we rely for security, that directs so much of what we think and do. It's this fear that compels us to make so many little, or large, compromises. If a sexual relationship is beginning to founder, we cast about in our minds for somebody who might provide the lifeboat. We go to inordinate lengths to fit in, to be popular, laughing at jokes we don't find funny, going to a party when, in all honesty, we'd prefer to stay at home. We bite our tongues and don't speak the truth, not usually to avoid hurting somebody's feelings, but to avoid rejection and isolation.

If we didn't fear loneliness or isolation, we wouldn't be so rocked by praise or blame, attention or indifference. We are highly attuned to the reactions of others. We are skilled in knowing how to live up to expectations, how to gain approval, appreciation, and attention. The *fear* of loneliness, if not the fact of it, directs how we lead our lives to a great extent. And yet we can never quite escape loneliness. Although we may not experience it as overtly or consciously painful, if we listen closely to our experience, we can detect the sound of loneliness playing continually, like the gentle, background drone of a bagpipe. By virtue of being human, we inevitably experience loneliness. My teacher, Sangharakshita, put it this way:

> The very fact of one's subjectivity – that one has a sense of ego, or separate self – means that one will always feel to some extent cut off from others. The mere fact that others are others means that you are isolated and therefore experience loneliness. If you are sufficiently mindful you will notice that subtle sense of loneliness in your experience all the time.[6]

We all evolve many strategies, some subtle, some not so subtle, to alleviate or deaden this pang of separation. But, as we shall see, a clear-sighted acknowledgement of our essential aloneness is where the spiritual life begins. According to Buddhism, such an acknowledgement is the precursor to liberation and joy.

In reflecting on the theme of loneliness for this book, I was surprised to realize to what extent it's such a predominant theme in music, painting, and literature. I don't know why I was so surprised. If loneliness is truly the theme of everyone, that theme will be everywhere present in the music we listen to, in the pictures we look at, in the books we read . . . And, after all, it's said that the arts were created by the god Pan, after his unsuccessful pursuit of a water nymph. Lonely and sexually frustrated, Pan sat on a river bank, fashioned a pipe from a reed (actually the transformed body of Syrinx, the water nymph in question), and played the blues.

If we listen carefully, we start to hear Pan's haunting, background music everywhere in the books, films, or paintings we look to for meaning – even in the books, films, or paintings we look to for escape. We can hear that music in the great tragic plays of Shakespeare – in *Hamlet* and *King Lear* – in the poetry of Philip Larkin, and in the dialogue of Harold Pinter. It provides the incidental music for every television detective show you care to name, with the cop or private investigator coming home, after a hard day at the crime scene, to an unstocked fridge and a non-existent private life. It's there in the soft-focus, sentimental landscape hanging on the wall of the inner-city living room.

Sometimes this background theme becomes the melody itself. Loneliness, for example, seems to be a major theme in many of Tennessee Williams' plays, his characters constantly searching for something or someone to help them make it through the night. 'I have always depended on the kindness of strangers', Williams' heroine Blanche du Bois flirtatiously, and famously, remarks as she attempts to hang on to her dignity and sanity in the face of overwhelming loneliness. And loneliness is one of the major themes of another American, Edward Hopper.

Edward Hopper, born in 1882, was a realist painter. His most famous and most widely reproduced painting is *Nighthawks*, a representation of three men and a woman glimpsed through the glass front of a bar diner, in what seems an otherwise deserted city, late at night. In his paintings, Hopper portrays the bleak architecture and seedy environments of launderettes, hotel rooms, gas stations, theatres, movie houses, bars, offices, and cafés. He shows men and women often isolated in stark rooms, absorbed in themselves, detached from their world and from one another.

The things that we might normally crop from a photo or a picture are Hopper's studies, studies that have their own desolate beauty: dull walls of brick and concrete; overgrown railway yards; dusty cars; deserted, windswept streets; strange, ugly buildings . . . Similarly, the characters he represents are involved in activities we might crop from our memories or our diaries, activities often on the periphery of a more conventionally interesting event or situation, activities that highlight the characters' loneliness. So Hopper gives us, for example, paintings of men and women sitting in a theatre between acts. One painting is actually called *Intermission*. The movie screen in another painting is only glimpsed at the edge of the canvas, while an usherette stands to one side, lost in a reverie. Hopper's characters seem disconnected from what's happening around them – idly absorbed in a book or magazine, say, or, frequently, lost in their own thoughts.

Hopper has been described as a painter of modern urban alienation. His paintings seem to illustrate the paradox that we can experience loneliness most intensely when we're surrounded by millions, that we can feel isolated at the same time as being visible to multitudes. His theatres, cinemas, launderettes, and restaurants are only nominally places of social contact. Everyone is turning inward. In the city, where everyone is under surveillance, sociability and community actually seem to decrease, and silence and introspection offer protection. In this context, the writer Richard Sennett gives the example of a large, open-plan office:

> This destruction of walls, office planners are quick to say, increases office efficiency, because when people are all day long visually exposed to one another, they are less likely to gossip and chat, more likely to keep to themselves.[7]

The loneliness of Hopper's characters, which often seems to move into isolation and depression, actually appears more pronounced when they're shown with one another. Many of us understand all too well this feeling of loneliness as it shades into isolation, a feeling we can experience even, or especially, when we're with others. Such a feeling can be accompanied by mental-health problems, like depression or chronic anxiety. In a state of depressed isolation, it can feel as if there is a fog or a veil existing between ourselves and others. We yearn to connect and break out of this isolation, but such an intense yearning often seems to perpetuate the problem. In extreme cases we can feel unreal. In *The Divided Self* the psychiatrist R.D. Laing describes the extreme and harrowing case of a schizophrenic girl who was so isolated that she hardly felt present at all. She described herself as 'the ghost of the weed garden'.[8]

One senses that more and more people these days are experiencing feelings of isolation, with the attendant mental-health issues. A superficial look at some statistics in the UK seem to bear this out. Figures from 2007 showed that children in Britain were three times more likely to live in single-parent households than they were in 1972, with a quarter of children now living with only one parent. The same figures reported that 7 million people lived alone in 2007, compared with 3 million in 1972. According to the NHS website, suicide is now the biggest killer of young men aged between eighteen and thirty-four, with an average of three deaths a day. And in 2008, according to a report in *The Observer*, 36 million prescriptions for antidepressants were issued, an increase of twenty-four per cent over the previous five years. For all the talk of 'community' in the media, it seems that, in Britain at least, people are becoming more isolated, more removed from a feeling of social connection.

But for all the sobering nature of such statistics, for all the problems that city life and the pressures of modern living can bring, the Buddhist perspective on all this is quite clear. These are extreme symptoms of a malaise as old as mankind. We can work to alleviate the pain of these symptoms, but to eradicate the deeper disease we must look to the human condition itself.

Like all great artists, Edward Hopper was interested in the deeper truths about human beings. He was far more than *just* a painter of modern, urban alienation. For one thing, his portraits of characters living in the countryside reveal them to be just as lonely as their city counterparts. There seems to be a search going on within the characters he represents, some attempt at an inward communion or connection, a connection that these characters cannot discover with one another.

In one of Hopper's paintings, *Excursion into Philosophy*, a man sits, hunched, on the side of a bed. Behind him, sleeping, lies a semi-naked woman. A discarded book lies next to the man and he's staring at a rectangle of sunlight projected onto the bedroom floor. The title of the picture almost seems a mockery. The man in the picture's obviously puzzled and despondent, divorced from any sense of meaning or understanding. The harsh sunlight in Hopper's pictures highlights the fact that his characters are alienated from one another, but it also highlights the fact that they're alienated from any enlightenment or understanding. The rectangle of light in *Excursion into Philosophy* seems to challenge the man on the bed to rise to some kind of illumination, but we can tell that he's unable to meet the challenge. He seems caught between the sensual world and the spiritual, unable to connect with either. In some of his last paintings Hopper depicts sunlight in an entirely empty room. In a sense, we now become the characters in his paintings. It is *we* who are offered the challenge.

Buddhism too offers a challenge. It challenges us both to recognize with courageous clarity our aloneness and to work to attenuate and overcome our alienation. Humankind's painful sense of aloneness and alienation and our capacity for deepening joy and illumination were the great themes of the Buddha. It was these themes that he addressed in his very first discourse, the discourse in which he introduced to the world the four noble truths.

Duhkha: the first noble truth

In his first noble truth the Buddha declared that existence was characterized by what he termed *duhkha*.[9] Duhkha is often translated simply as 'suffering', which can give a rather misleading impression. The Buddha was not saying that life was essentially miserable under all circumstances. To understand what the first noble truth did actually mean, it's worthwhile briefly examining the context out of which this teaching arose.

At the time of the Buddha, 2,500 years ago, much of India was changing. The population had increased significantly, more of society was under the rule of monarchs, and there was great growth in cities and towns, which had become centres of industry and trade. With all this change and expansion came a change also in how many people worked. More and more people were specializing in different trades – there were wood-workers, iron-workers, leather-workers, painters, ivory-workers, cooks, garment-makers . . . There was a host of different professions serving the royal courts, as well as many actors, tavern-keepers, singers, courtesans, and dancers who kept everyone entertained. This specialization was new and very different from traditional village life, and with it came a growing sense of individualism. In traditional village life, people had tended to resemble one another to a far greater extent. There was little differentiation of task and status; the collective life of the tribe was the important thing. But specialization gave everybody something that *individualized* them. So with specialization came differentiation and individualism – and something else too: an uneasy sense of essential separateness . . .

As the scholar Trevor Ling put it in *The Buddha*, his account of the social and political background to the Buddha's life and teaching:

> the transition which many people were then
> experiencing from the familiar, small-scale society of
> the old tribal republics to the strange, large-scale and
> consequently more impersonal, bleaker life of the new
> monarchical state, was accompanied by a psychological
> malaise, a heightened sense of dissatisfaction with
> life as it had to be lived. It was this malaise which the
> Buddha was to take as his starting-point of his analysis
> of the human condition, calling it dukkha.[10]

Duhkha had always been present in the human heart but, at a time when a more binding, intimate society was giving way to a more anonymous and less self-assured one, people generally were becoming more aware of this underlying dissatisfaction within their experience. What the Buddha did was to draw attention to that uneasiness, to articulate human beings' essential feeling of isolation and dissatisfaction, and to show that this feeling was universal. The particular conditions existing around the time of the Buddha meant that many people's hearts were ready to receive the Buddha's message. When the Buddha stated, in his first noble truth, that life was characterized by duhkha, he was pointing to a tangible experience that many people could relate to.

So to translate the term simply as 'suffering' does not fully convey the experience to which the Buddha was referring. We might want to consider some other words that are pertinent to the theme of this book, and that might help convey the meaning of duhkha: 'lack', for example, 'inauthenticity', 'disconnectedness', 'alienation', 'separation', 'dissatisfaction', 'loneliness', 'isolation', 'incompleteness' . . . When I was first becoming interested in Buddhism, I was very struck by an editorial in a Buddhist magazine that described our human condition and the Buddhist response to it in this way:

> None of us is complete; more or less by chance,
> we are tossed up by our conditioning – biological,
> psychological, social, and cultural – as partial beings.
> Our future lies in each one of us making something of
> him or herself; making of that miscellaneous bundle
> of conditionings a happy, free, clear-minded and
> emotionally radiant individual.[11]

'None of us is complete.' It was this phrase that particularly leapt out at me when I first read the editorial. We are not born into completeness. We are disconnected, separate, and incomplete, and we yearn for connection and completeness. This sense of *lack* has nothing to do with original sin. It is the stage our human consciousness has reached, a stage in human evolution. The Buddha said that we can evolve further but, to do that, we must first acknowledge our sense of painful isolation.

Duhkha, stated the Buddha, is the starting point of the spiritual life. With the first noble truth, the declaration that life is characterized by duhkha, the Buddha gave expression to, and clarified, a feeling that otherwise may have remained inarticulate and only semi-acknowledged, a feeling individuals might otherwise have thought was particular to themselves. I remember very well those periods in my adolescence and early twenties when I experienced strong feelings of alienation and isolation. I felt as if I was somehow different, misunderstood, an outsider, the square peg in the round hole, unable to connect with those around me, the *victim*. One of the many advantages of coming across the Buddha's teaching early on in my life was the realization that such feelings were, to a greater or lesser extent, universal. The Buddha was asking me – as he asks all those who are willing – to listen out for the sound of Pan's pipe; not to run from that lonely, haunting music, but to let it sound clearly; and to understand that, yes, it really is the theme of everyone.

Craving: the second noble truth

The reason for our continuing experience of duhkha, according to the Buddha, is craving. This is the second of the Buddha's four noble truths. The word for 'craving' in Pali is *tanha*, a very strong word that connotes thirst or drought. As deep as our sense of isolation and separateness is our yearning to overcome that separateness. So entangled are tanha and duhkha that it's difficult to see where one stops and the other begins. We crave an end to isolation, yearn to overcome our deep sense of incompleteness and loneliness, but this craving almost invariably perpetuates our isolation. Yet we can't just destroy craving. We are desiring beings. The problem is that the things we tend to habitually crave are not the things that cure the basic existential malaise. They don't alleviate our painful sense of separate selfhood. In fact, they usually perpetuate the problem. It's as if, suffering from terrible thirst, we drink sea water, which makes us thirstier still.

We instinctively reach for pleasurable sensations to take the pain out of our experience of separateness. Usually the pleasure we seek is immediate and not particularly subtle: food, sex, drink, fantasy, television . . . It's not that any of these things are necessarily harmful in themselves. Food, for example, is just food. It's just that we habitually rely on such things to attenuate our sense of duhkha. Thus we tend to set up a cycle of addiction, a habitual and repetitive need to replicate the conditions that give us pleasure and remove our sense of lack or loneliness. For a while such pleasures take the sting from our experience. They seem to work. But when that pleasure evaporates, as it inevitably will, we once again experience the sting of duhkha, sometimes even more strongly, and we crave more of that pleasure. In this way our lives tend towards the cyclic, the habitual, and the addictive. 'Addictive' may seem a strong word to use here but, if we reflect on our attempts to give up something we've relied on for years for pleasure and security (smoking, for example), we might be more convinced of the word's appropriateness.

For some years I taught meditation at the prison in Norwich. Many of the prisoners I taught were there for drug-related offences, and they didn't need to be persuaded of the truth of the Buddha's teaching on craving. I remember one prisoner in particular, a very articulate and intelligent man who'd been addicted to heroin from a very young age, talking to me about how his addiction had kept him isolated from others. He told me, for example, that if I'd come into his cell when he'd been in the grip of his addiction, his overriding reaction would have been thinking how to steal my jacket and how much he'd be able to get for it in order to help fuel his habit. I would have become merely a means to satisfy his craving.

Samsara is the word used in Buddhism to describe the cyclic, addictive nature of our existence. According to Buddhism, our deep craving and sense of separate selfhood have kept us trapped in this cycle for lifetime after lifetime. Samsara is also maintained by ideas, views, thoughts, fantasies, and ideologies that might seem to offer a way out of our painful state but, in the end, merely reinforce our dependency and sense of isolation. Materialism and consumerism, for example, keep the wheel of samsara rolling while promising wholeness and completeness. Take, for example, this advertisement for the perfume known, rather ironically, as 'Samsara':

> Samsara is the symbol of harmony, of absolute osmosis
> between a woman and her perfume. It is a spiritual
> voyage leading to serenity and inner contemplation . . .
> The stopper evokes the eye of Buddha, a symbol of
> meditation which leads to detachment and supreme
> enlightenment.[12]

And it's only £56.50 a bottle.

When I was thinking of an image to encapsulate samsara, this cycle of isolation and yearning, I remembered a film I saw years ago called *They Shoot Horses, Don't They?* The film, based on a novel by Horace McCoy, is set during the American Depression and concerns two drifters, Robert and Gloria, film extras who, desperate and lonely, pair up to enter a dance marathon. Dance marathons were gruelling affairs, endurance contests lasting several weeks in which the contestants would be required to keep dancing day and night, with a ten-minute break every two hours. The winners would be the last couple left standing. Popular in the 1920s and 1930s, these contests could attract huge audiences. In the film, Rocky, the master of ceremonies, whips up the audience and galvanizes the contestants with dreams of fame, romance, and fortune:

19

Yowza! Yowza! Yowza! Welcome to the dance of
destiny, ladies and gentlemen. Around and around
and around we go and we're only beginning folks,
only beginning! On and on and on and when will it
stop? When will it end? When? Only when the last
two of these wonderful, starry-eyed kids are left . . .[13]

And so we watch as the wonderful, starry-eyed kids battle
exhaustion and despair. Some of the luckier ones are sponsored
by a local company and get some clean clothes with the sponsor's
name on the back. Others perform little acts for a bit of extra
money. Many hope that they'll be spotted by a Hollywood talent
scout. All hope that they'll last the duration and win the cash prize
for last couple standing. The characters are lost and seem very
lonely. In the film, a young woman who's close to a breakdown
takes Robert to a secluded part of the dance hall. As they tear
off each other's clothes, the girl asks Robert to tell her things,
talk to her, tell her where he's from, what his father did, about
his family . . . And as the gruelling marathon continues, the MC
conjures up a false world of glamour, heroism, and sentimental
drama. The audience begins to swell, and the arena is visited by
various curious celebrities. Gloria is tired of the whole tawdry
merry-go-round:

'I'm sick of this,' Gloria said. 'I'm sick of looking at
celebrities and I'm sick of doing the same thing over
and over again.'[14]

Every so often, to spice up the marathon, there's a 'derby'. In
this, the already exhausted couples are asked to race around the
perimeter of the hall for a set period, and the couple who come
in last is eliminated. This is the most powerful image in the film
and it's the one that really stuck with me. The remaining couples,

close to physical and mental collapse, their eyes staring and hollow, haul each other round the arena, strain every muscle to remain upright and conscious, circle the hall, chase the dream . . .

It's a story of unremitting bleakness. Gloria has seen through the whole false dream and her attitude becomes increasingly cynical and despairing. In the end she wants off the merry-go-round. She asks her partner to kill her – and Robert obliges. In the book, the boy is sentenced to death. End of story. I'm not sure why the film had such a strong effect on me when I first saw it. Perhaps it was because I could relate to the total disillusionment of the two main characters. It didn't seem like a story applicable only to America or the American Depression. It felt current. The tragedy of the two main characters is that they look at the world around them and see nothing there to inspire or sustain them – only empty promises and false dreams, which serve merely to reinforce their loneliness and suffering. Nor do they have any sense of their own inner resources. Gloria especially is full of self-hatred. Yet characters like Gloria and Robert may be the kind of people who are most ready to hear the Buddha's teaching. Similarly today, it is often those of us who are most disillusioned with aspects of society who are most ready to respond to the truths the Buddha expounded, truths that point beyond despair and isolation.

Nirvana: the third noble truth

In his third noble truth, the Buddha declared that there is a state of being in which duhkha is overcome, in which isolation is transcended. Such a state, which the Buddha called *nirvana*, is synonymous with a state of egolessness. I quoted Sangharakshita as saying that, if we have an ego or separate self, loneliness and isolation will be subtly present in our experience all the time. In going beyond the ego, we also go beyond loneliness and isolation. But breaking out of isolation is not like breaking through some imagined finishing tape. The practice of Buddhism is designed to gradually weaken the power of the ego, so, if our practice of Buddhism is effective, our sense of isolation will also be gradually attenuated. We will slowly begin to relate to others in a more authentic and compassionate way. Our painful sense of separateness will gradually diminish.

In the process of moving from samsara to nirvana, the nature of our craving and desire also gradually changes. As we've seen, we are desiring beings. We can't just suddenly destroy desire, although, particularly in the early days of the spiritual life, impatient and idealistic, this is precisely what some of us attempt to do. Premature and wilful vows of celibacy, lifelong vows to never touch a drop of alcohol, the renunciation of the guitar and the entire record collection . . . Such activities may be a necessary stage that we have to go through, and we can certainly learn from them, but I don't think they're particularly effective in a spiritual sense. I shudder now at the memories of those bonfires, upon which possessions, books, and diaries went up in flames, in the vain hope that a radiant, new being would immediately spring from the ashes, his old loves and passions things of the past. (How I'd love to retrieve my diary for 1972, the facsimile copy of the Book of Kells, and my letters from Michael Palin, John Cleese, and Spike Milligan . . .) No, we can't destroy desire, but what we can do is gradually move our desires in the direction of a more wholesome, and realizable, dream. We can begin to channel our craving towards the realization of our own authentic welfare and the welfare of others. Buddhism challenges us to get our passions behind our spiritual practice, to yearn for truth and beauty and kindness as strongly as we have yearned, in the past, for comfort and unconsciousness.

Samsara is that cyclic way of being in which our isolation is actually perpetuated by the mistaken belief that it can be removed by grasping at comfort, happiness, and security outside ourselves. The Buddha taught that we must cease to yearn for happiness outside ourselves and begin to trust the potential for nirvana that lies within us. The journey from samsara towards nirvana involves a passionate and deepening desire for a certain kind of self-sufficiency.

When we read of the lives of various Buddhist saints and teachers, it's often this self-sufficiency that we are struck by. These teachers, hermits, and yogis are no longer yearning for comfort, pleasure, and security from the outside world. Take, for example, the famous Tibetan hermit and yogi Milarepa, who lived in the eleventh century AD and whose life and adventures inspired so much devotion among the Tibetan people. In paintings he is often shown outside his cave in the Himalayan mountains wearing only a light cotton robe or loincloth. He is happy in these pictures, often singing for joy. Sometimes he is portrayed with a green body, the result of an exclusive diet of nettles. Milarepa has nothing and wants nothing. Admittedly, he has a cooking pot but, at one point, it gets broken, merely inspiring him to sing a song about the impermanent nature of all things. He also has his robe, of course, but Milarepa never seems particularly attached to his robe. Quite literally – as it tends to get blown away by the fierce wind. The attempts by his family and friends to give him trousers or a loincloth to cover his nakedness only serve to persuade the yogi to deliver a lecture on the naked truth or naked reality or the true nature of shame. He is blissfully happy in his solitude, he revels in his aloneness, and he finds his extremely ascetic life bracing and energizing. Compare the image of Milarepa sitting quietly and happily at the mouth of his cave to the image of the couples desperately racing round and round the perimeter of the dance hall in *They Shoot Horses, Don't They?* and we have a sense of the essential difference between samsara and nirvana. The couples in the marathon are pursuing hope and security outside themselves, and this drives them in tragic circles. Milarepa has stopped chasing things. He has found the end to isolation and duhkha within his own heart.

Can the example of Milarepa really inspire us? His life seems so remote from our own. Can we really imagine ourselves sitting outside an isolated Himalayan cave in our underwear, happily self-contained, iPod lost in an avalanche, mobile phone buried under six feet of snow, sipping nettle soup and singing for joy? But the life of Milarepa, whom we'll meet again in the next chapter, offers us an alternative to all the shabby dreams and goals we've been asked to invest in. We may not spend much time up a literal mountain side, but Milarepa remains an inspiration, challenging us to gradually loosen our tight hold on our possessions, to value solitude that little bit more, to become that little bit more self-contained and self-reliant. Just as a Buddhist life helps us to gradually attenuate the ego, so too it helps us begin to value and develop the kind of qualities that Milarepa embodies.

The first Buddhist retreat I went on took place in a youth hostel in Gairloch on the west coast of Scotland. It took place over Christmas and New Year in the midst of what seemed like a perpetual blizzard. The retreat, which was led by two ordained Buddhists, Ajita and Uttara, was dedicated to Milarepa and involved quite a lot of meditation. We were grouped around a huge log that acted as a shrine. On one side of me sat Uttara, dark-haired and intense, meditating with a frown of concentration. On the other side sat Ajita. He seemed happy and at ease, smiling gently. The snow lashed against the windows of the shrine room as we sat quietly concentrating on the breath. The meditations were punctuated with readings from Milarepa's life, or from his songs:

I am a man who cares not what may happen.
I am an alms beggar who has no food,
A nude hermit without clothes,
A beggar without jewels.
I have no place to lay my head;
I am the one who never thinks of external objects –
The master of all yogic action.

Like a madman, I am happy if death comes:
I have nothing and want nought.[15]

It was after this retreat at Gairloch that I went on my first solitary retreat. It was both a magical and a very painful time. On my walks through the Highland winter, I gradually came to some painful decisions. At the end of the retreat I decided to move into a Buddhist community. I couldn't say that it was Milarepa who inspired me to do all this, but the example of the cotton-clad yogi was certainly one of the important conditioning factors in convincing me that there could be a different way to live, that a life of simplicity, community, and increasing self-sufficiency was a life worth aiming for. It was his example that helped to persuade me I could begin to truly trust myself and my potential for change.

The path: the fourth noble truth

The fourth of the Buddha's great truths is that there is a path leading from samsara to nirvana. This is the Buddha's noble eightfold path, which, in very general terms, comprises the vast range of Buddhist practices that lead from duhkha and isolation to freedom. The Buddhist path is a way of developing ever deeper levels of positive emotion. For example, in practising generosity, we generate the positive state of mind to more effectively meditate.

In turn, an effective meditation practice deepens our practice of generosity, and so on. The path, according to Sangharakshita,

> symbolizes the creative mind, or the whole process of cumulative, as distinct from reactive, conditionality. It works on the principle not of round and round, but of up and up.[16]

As Buddhists we commit ourselves to a way of being that is augmentative and creative in nature, as opposed to the cyclic and repetitive behaviour that keeps us firmly embedded in samsara.

Positive emotion is that which frees us from isolation and loneliness (although, as we shall see, a sense of loneliness *may* initially become accentuated when we first commit ourselves to the Buddhist path). Negative emotions, such as hatred, jealousy, self-loathing, cruelty, and so on, isolate us from others. The more extreme the negative emotion, the more isolated we feel. The Buddhist writer Jack Kornfield cites a serial killer who described himself as 'the loneliest man in the world'.[17] Shakespeare's arch villain, Richard III, on the eve of battle, having murdered all his enemies, laments his isolation and loneliness, realizing that there will be nobody in the world who will miss him when he's gone. Much positive emotion – tranquillity, equanimity, bliss – involves a certain self-sufficiency. But, if we reflect, we'll notice that most positive emotion – compassion, for example, generosity, kindness – is *connecting* emotion, social emotion, and other-regarding.

So, in following the Buddhist path, in attempting to consistently generate positive states of mind, a Buddhist practises with and for others. In working together with like-minded people on the basis of shared ideals, in practising spiritual friendship, in engaging in compassionate activity, we are taken out of mere self-concern and challenged to become more altruistic and outward-looking. Yet, as well as practising with others, the Buddhist tradition (and this may seem paradoxical given the connecting, social, and other-regarding nature of what we're trying to create) emphasizes another mode of training in order to generate positive emotion: a Buddhist must also train in the capacity to be alone.

3

'Trust Thyself'

The Capacity to Be Alone

*All the unhappiness of man stems from one thing only: that
he is incapable of staying quietly in his room.*[18]

Blaise Pascal

'Let it cut more deep . . .'

We are essentially alone. You can never be certain what I'm
thinking and I can never be certain what you're thinking. We
dream alone, we are born alone, and we die alone. One of the
reasons we fear death so much is that it is a journey we take without
friends, family, or loved ones. No amount of friendship or love
can remove our essential aloneness. Indeed, as Sangharakshita
says, an honest and intimate friendship can even highlight our
essential separateness:

> The better you know someone and the more time
> you spend with them, the more you realize they are
> fundamentally different and ultimately separate from
> you . . . In the end you don't understand how it feels
> to be them, and nor can they understand how it feels
> to be you. So, although you may live for years side by

side with someone who is very dear to you, your very closeness may help you to see that you are really on your own.[19]

Buddhism challenges us to address our loneliness and isolation by facing up to it, by ceasing to run from it. As we've seen, our habitual responses to duhkha tend to the cyclic and addictive. We seek to alleviate feelings of isolation and emptiness with a quick fix: obsessive thinking, fantasy, company, food . . . But this never quite solves the problem, compelling us to seek further comfort. It can seem very difficult just to sit with a sense of loneliness and emptiness and not reach for the usual reassurances. Yet sitting with tension in this way is where the Buddhist path begins.

As we've seen, the Buddhist path is creative, rather than reactive, augmentative, rather than cyclic in nature. The development of positive emotion creates the conditions for experiencing further and deeper levels of positive emotion, which, in turn, give rise to the possibility of even *more* refined states of positivity. So, rather than being caught up in the cycle of desire and reactivity to which our habits and addictive behaviour constrain us, if our Buddhist practice is effective, we will find ourselves, rather, on a *spiral* path, a path which 'works on the principle not of round and round, but of up and up'.[20] One of the formulations of the Buddhist path is what's called the *positive nidana chain*. The positive nidana chain is a progressive series of links that demonstrates the nature of the creative mind, and the ever-increasing levels of positivity to which we have access as our Buddhist practice deepens. The first link on this spiral path is duhkha, the fact of our essential separate selfhood. An *awareness* of duhkha, which involves, among other things, a courageous acknowledgement of our aloneness, is the launching pad for the Buddhist journey.

A painful sense of isolation or loneliness may be one of the things that compels us to seek a spiritual life. For some of us, the first stages of that spiritual journey may offer us immediate rewards in terms of new connections and friendships. For others, however, our sense of loneliness might even be accentuated. We may find it necessary, for example, to break with a group that has hitherto provided our comfort and support. We may find that, with certain old acquaintances, we're increasingly unable to be ourselves or to relate meaningfully, and that we need to move on from those old acquaintances and find kindred spirits. Such a break doesn't have to be final or irrevocable, but the point is that there's often a painful period after we've left an old way of life behind, and before we've discovered a new one, which calls for patience and courage in the face of loneliness. One of the loneliest times of my own life was the period when I first moved into a Buddhist community. I'd burnt my bridges and there was no going back, at least not for the time being, but I missed my friends and family and, in that period before making new, significant friendships, loneliness blazed in my heart like a fire. Yet, if we allow it to, such loneliness can be a fire of transformation.

As we'll see in the last chapter, the Buddha stressed the importance of spiritual friendship and community. Yet, in one of his final teachings, as he was dying, he exhorted his disciples to

> be islands unto yourselves, refuges unto yourselves,
> seeking no external refuge; with the Dhamma [the
> Buddha's teaching] as your island, the Dhamma as
> your refuge, seeking no other refuge.[21]

The example and teaching of the Buddha and the Buddhist spiritual community are indispensable to the Buddhist path. But here the Buddha was saying that we have to tread that path for ourselves. We have to be our own saviours.

Buddhism asks us to let go of our habitual distractions and addictions, and foster a capacity to be alone. And if we practise effectively, then we begin to find that this sense of aloneness becomes more and more bracing and refreshing. We begin to experience the discomfort as growing pains. We begin to sit easier with it all. Initially, on our first solitary retreat, for example, our sense of loneliness may be quite acute. But this isn't (necessarily) a problem. It's as if we're detoxing, going against our habitual addictive patterns. When I first became involved in Buddhism I wanted immediate results. I wanted to escape pain and loneliness, and experience pleasure and relief. It took me a while to realize that I needed to stop running from my own loneliness, that running in this way was actually just increasing my painful states of mind. As the poet Hafiz put it:

> Don't surrender your loneliness so quickly.
> let it cut more deep.
> Let it ferment and season you
> as few human or even divine ingredients can.[22]

The capacity to be alone

One of the ways in which we surrender our loneliness, of course, is by seeking out other people as soon as the discomfort begins to kick in. Companionship, love, and friendship are all necessary in our lives, but we too easily look towards others for comfort or reassurance. Distrusting our capacity to be alone, we too quickly look to others to save us, often from ourselves. And, as a consequence of our self-esteem so readily relying on the approval and reassurance of others, we become addicted to other people. The Jesuit writer, Anthony de Mello, whose thinking was influenced by Eastern religion, is refreshingly blunt about our addiction to others:

you became cravenly dependent on others and you lost your freedom. Others now have the power to make you happy or miserable. You crave your drugs, but as much as you hate the suffering that this involves, you find yourself completely helpless. There is never a minute when, consciously or unconsciously, you are not aware or attuned to the reactions of others, marching to the beat of their drums.[23]

An awareness of the extent to which we rely on others for our self-esteem is a first step towards freeing ourselves from that dependency. Freeing ourselves is difficult because it's a dependency that is celebrated everywhere in our society. The pressure to be an even number, for example, is overwhelming. From the age of about twelve, I was semi-aware of the pressure to have a girlfriend. I even invented one when Raymond Macmillan asked me:

'Do you have a girlfriend?'
'Yes.'
'What's her name?'
'Jane.'
'Jane who?'
'Jane . . . de la Tour.'

I don't know why I came up with such an unusual surname. I suppose I panicked and I remember Raymond giving me a very suspicious glance. Realizing that to maintain the lie might create more problems than it might solve, the next time Raymond asked me about Jane, I gave a world-weary shrug as if to say it had all folded, as these things tend to do. I was single again. But being single, even then, was not a state to be desired. The loner in our society is the loser, the odd number, the guy on the park bench who

33

looks enviously at the couple laughing and dancing among the buttercups and who curses himself for not having administered the requisite deodorant. (Similarly, the woman on the park bench who has failed to spray herself with Samsara perfume.) How much misery we can cause ourselves in this yearning for a partner, this quest to find someone who can take the pain away, who can make us socially acceptable. Because that's part of the deal, to be able to say that we're part of an even number, that we're not a failure in the eyes of society.

I'd like to emphasize again that I'm not denying the importance of friendship or our relationships with others. Most of my Buddhist friends are in sexual relationships. My teacher has stressed the importance of having good relations with one's family. The Buddhist life is a life of altruism and community. Yet this book is about solitude and the importance of the capacity to be alone within Buddhism. Solitude is not very often championed. The fact is that we tend to rely on friends, family, and lovers to the *exclusion* of being with ourselves. And a certain *kind* of romantic relationship, sentimental and not always based on maturity, or any kind of clear-sightedness, is often presented as the true solution to loneliness. How many films have you seen where the hero or heroine, in the closing scene, cheerfully walks towards the sunset on their own?

In his book *Solitude*, Anthony Storr argues that the capacity to be alone is undervalued. Psychological health, he says, is too easily equated with the ability to form loving relationships, connections, and friendships. And, although these *are* means of evaluating psychological health, they are not the only criteria:

> Many ordinary interests, and the majority of creative
> pursuits involving real originality, continue without
> involving relationships. It seems to me that what
> goes on in the human being when he is by himself

is as important as what happens in his interactions
with other people . . . Two opposing drives operate
throughout life: the drive for companionship, love,
and everything else which brings us close to our
fellow men, and the drive toward being independent,
separate, and autonomous.[24]

He goes on to say that, if we attended only to certain psychoanalytic
schools of thought, we would be forced to conclude that 'none of
us have validity as isolated individuals.'[25] Storr gives examples
of artistic men and women (including Beatrix Potter, Edward
Lear, Rudyard Kipling, and Anthony Trollope) whose solitude
and isolation were prerequisites for their creativity. He also
mentions how, in old age, emotional dependence tends to decline,
partly, perhaps, as a preparation for death. And, interestingly,
Storr makes the point that it's only since the decline of a shared
religion that so much weight has been placed on interpersonal
relationships. This implies that the capacity to be alone is an
essential part of a spiritual life. It's certainly true of Buddhism.

Whether on retreat, travelling on our own, standing at a bus
stop, sitting in our room, gardening, cooking, or just lying in
bed, Buddhism challenges us to train ourselves to be more and
more at ease in our own company; to try and be with ourselves
without distraction. But one of the things that greatly hinders our
capacity to be alone is a (particularly Western) tendency to give
ourselves a hard time. This can manifest as lack of self-esteem,
harsh self-criticism, self-hatred, and so on. Quite a few American
writers on Buddhism have cited the occasion, during a Buddhist
conference, when the Dalai Lama was amazed at the number of
Western Buddhists who confessed to a lack of self-esteem. 'Do *you*
have this?' he would ask another Western delegate who would
invariably reply in the affirmative. Perhaps such self-hatred
and lack of self-esteem originates with the doctrine of original

sin, which still lurks in the Western psyche. In a way, it doesn't matter where it originates. All that matters is that we deal with it effectively because, if we're not on good terms with ourselves, the Buddhist path and our capacity to be alone become very problematic.

The first thing is to acknowledge that self-hatred isn't a virtue. I had a friend who would regularly receive feedback that she was an exceptionally kind and generous person, but that she wasn't very kind to herself. Eventually I realized that this trait persisted because she was somehow *proud* of the fact that she wasn't kind to herself, proud of the fact that basically she didn't like herself very much. She seemed to see it as some kind of proof of an altruistic attitude. It wasn't. Self-hatred is no different from any other kind of hatred. What's more, if we give ourselves an unnecessarily harsh time for, say, having sexual fantasies, then those sexual fantasies will mysteriously multiply. It's not so mysterious actually. If we are giving ourselves a harsh and unpleasant dressing down, why should it come as a surprise when we want to fly from ourselves into the comforting arms of another, even if only in fantasy? Self-hatred reinforces the cycle of yearning and addiction and actually propels us towards others.

What do we do with this carping, cruel, and overcritical voice, which is constantly telling us that we don't come up to scratch, that we *must* do better, that we're never quite good enough, even that there's something fundamentally *wrong* with us? We can't respond with harshness. It only seems to perpetuate the difficulty.

A kindly, even amused, awareness is often the way forward. In meditation, for example, we may experience a vague sense of discomfort and depression. As we become more aware, we may locate a harsh, judgemental, and critical voice that has arisen in response to our distracted mind, and is the source of our discomfort. We don't need to take this voice seriously. We can just treat it as another distraction – and try not to judge the judging voice! We should let such voices, feelings, and thoughts come and go. If we're aware of them, they tend to just play themselves out. And they get easier to deal with. Sometimes it's useful to characterize such thoughts, for ease of identification. I've been working on this chapter of the book as part of a three-week solitary retreat and, on the first few days here, I noticed an underlying discomfort in my mind. The discomfort, I began to realize, was originating from a familiar carping voice, so I gave the voice a personality. Normally the voice belongs to a particularly severe schoolteacher but, on this occasion, I decided to give it to a small, military man with a pot belly and a waxed moustache. I called him Dress Sergeant. He had a red face and a tight, red military tunic as worn in the days of Queen Victoria and, as Dress Sergeant trotted behind me, he addressed me thus:

> Trouble with you, lad, is you're too timid. You're
> walking the same route again, aren't you? You always
> come this way because you're basically timid. That's
> what I think. Same when you swim in the sea. You
> should swim out to the rocks. Test yourself. You need
> to live lad. You've never really lived! And while we're
> at it, I don't think you're working hard enough on your
> writing. You've got to keep that nose to the grindstone.
> This isn't a holiday you know, lad . . .

And on and on . . . But slowly, although his face got redder, and his tunic tighter, and although he tried to yell louder and louder in order to be heard, the voice gradually died down. Two days ago, I was swimming in the sea when Dress Sergeant's head exploded in a shower of bloody sparks and he was gone. Only his waxed moustache was left bobbing poignantly on the surface of the waves. Dress Sergeant will return but I'm taking him and his like less seriously these days. These harsh, self-critical thoughts and voices, although they can seem to go very deep, are ephemeral. They come and go like clouds. Because we can experience them with such force, however, we can mistrust our own minds. We can become convinced that, deep down, we are basically bad. This is not the case. In fact, according to Buddhism, in a very fundamental way, the opposite is the case.

The *Metta Bhavana*, or development of loving-kindness, meditation practice is a very effective way of dealing with self-hatred. Through visualizing images, repeating a simple phrase, or by some other means, we generate feelings of kindness firstly towards ourselves, then towards a good friend, a relative stranger, and somebody we normally dislike, and then we extend the feelings of love to everybody we can imagine. I tend to try and get in touch with a sense of calmness and relaxation, become aware of my breathing and then repeat such phrases as 'May I be well. May I be happy. May I wake up.' I use the phrases sparingly and try and feel them sincerely in my heart. I then imagine the people in the consequent stages, breathing with me as I address the phrases to them. As well as effectively dealing with our tendency to self-hatred, the Metta Bhavana takes us beyond self-concern to empathize with others – beings, like ourselves, of limitless potential.

As we continue to practise the Metta Bhavana, and begin to feel more at ease with developing love towards ourselves in the first stage of the meditation, it will become increasingly apparent that the capacity to be alone doesn't just involve some kind of stoical acceptance of what is basically second best. It's not a matter of us finding it difficult to connect with others so, by default, going for the less attractive option. The capacity to be alone involves a positive delight in our own company. Here's a poem by Derek Walcott that I find particularly useful:

Love after Love

The time will come
when, with elation,
you will greet yourself arriving
at your own door, in your own mirror,
and each will smile at the other's welcome

and say, sit here. Eat.
You will love again the stranger who was your self.
Give wine. Give bread. Give back your heart
to itself, to the stranger who has loved you

all your life, whom you have ignored
for another, who knows you by heart.
Take down the love letters from the bookshelf,

the photographs, the desperate notes,
Peel your own image from the mirror.
Sit. Feast on your life.[26]

Who do we sleep with every night and have done since we were born? Who do we sit down to eat with at every meal? Who is our constant companion for richer, for poorer, in sickness and in health? Who do we visit the toilet with on a frequent basis every day? Who do we spend our entire lives with? Who will we eventually die with? It seems vital that we have a loving relationship with this person. One of the ways in which we can achieve this is through the Buddhist practice of mindfulness, by trying to bring an undistracted and kindly awareness to all the activities of our lives – to the meals, the washing up, the cups of tea, the showers, the reading, the standing at the bus stop, the looking in the mirror . . . There is a sensual, pleasurable aspect to mindfulness that perhaps is not emphasized enough. We miss a lot of enjoyment in jumping from distraction to distraction. But by mindfully delighting in our daily activities, including the many, many things we do on our own, we can truly begin to feast on our lives.

If we practise mindfulness in a regular and consistent way, we may begin to rediscover the sense of delight in the world around us that is often a characteristic of childhood. In a certain way, objects, animals, and our environment were a source of more importance when we were children, and our relationships with others perhaps not quite so all-consuming. We relied on friends, siblings, and parents, of course, but perhaps we also had a more spontaneous self-sufficiency, a capacity to be alone, an ability to become absorbed in activities without the adult compulsion to be part of an even number. Especially on retreat we may begin to rediscover the worlds of frogs, pebbles, colours, birds, flowers, newts, ponds, and tree-climbing. We may also begin to develop that unselfconscious sense of play that is such a feature of childhood. Such a sense of play and delight can also begin to inform all the activities we perform on our own – the travelling, the walking, the eating out – without that enjoyment being marred by the sense that such an activity can only truly be enjoyed with a companion.

Fostering the capacity to be alone isn't the same thing as self-indulgence or self-obsession. It's learning to hold all that we do, and all that we think, in the awareness we've been talking about. This awareness is not a neutral, colourless thing. There is something about true awareness or mindfulness that is *essentially* kindly and compassionate, and loving ourselves in this way is not being weak or limp. With a kindly awareness we can't go wrong. We can get up at 5 a.m. and meditate. We can exist on a diet of nettles if need be. It's when we start to become harsh with ourselves, too wilful or goal-orientated, that the problems begin. It's so important that we are kind to our mind. And when we are kind to our mind, it will be kind to us and we will progress in leaps and bounds.

Training in the capacity to be alone is about learning to be more and more at *ease* with your aloneness. It is essentially about trusting yourself, about seeing that this person you spend your life with really is worth the effort. 'Trust thyself', said the American writer and sage, Emerson, in his essay 'Self-Reliance'. 'Every heart vibrates to that iron string.'[27] The next stage in the spiral path of positive nidanas, or links, to which we've referred, following on from duhkha, is faith. In terms of the theme of this book, you could see faith as a growing confidence in your capacity to be on your own, without distraction. In other words, a kindly awareness and recognition of duhkha, an ability to be seasoned by your loneliness and discomfort without running to habitual comforts, gives rise to confidence. Part of this confidence consists in beginning to realize the extent to which you can rely on your own inner resources (and the extent to which you've chased pleasure and comfort outside yourself in the past). You begin to have a growing faith in your own potential. This isn't blind faith or a kind of unsubstantiated hope or belief, but a genuine confidence in your ability to change. You might even have the occasional glimpse of yourself as a future Milarepa or Buddha. After all, according to Buddhism, Milarepa and the Buddha represent the fundamental essence of your nature. Such fundamental purity is the very opposite of original sin, something to reflect on when Dress Sergeant is yelling at you.

A room with a view

The poet Philip Larkin often reflected on the themes of solitude and loneliness in his work. In 'Vers de société', for example, he writes about receiving an invitation to a dinner party. He reflects how hard it is to be alone, how much of life is spent filled with such engagements, how solitude is seen as selfish and virtue seen as necessarily 'social'. Initially inclined to refuse the invitation, he further reflects on the difficulties of solitude (how, for example, it can throw up feelings of failure and remorse), then caves in and accepts the invitation. In another poem, 'Best Society', he reflects on childhood solitude and how it seemed a 'plentiful and obvious thing'. However, in later life, he goes on to consider, solitude becomes more problematic and harder to achieve. The social pressures mount and, again, a worthwhile and virtuous life is associated entirely with one's relationships with others. Nevertheless, despite the pressures, Larkin decides to retire to his room. The poem ends:

> Viciously, then, I lock my door.
> The gas-fire breathes. The wind outside
> Ushers in evening rain. Once more
> Uncontradicting solitude
> Supports me in its giant palm;
> And like a sea-anemone
> Or simple snail, there cautiously
> Unfolds, emerges what I am.[28]

I like the word 'viciously'. Given the busy nature of most of our lives, our solitude really has to be fought for. And it's not just external social pressures we have to combat, but our own enormous tendency to distract ourselves from any kind of authentic or meaningful relationship with ourselves. It can take a surprising amount of effort to lock our door and stay in our room. Locking our door on the outside world and retreating to our room, of course, is not necessarily a positive thing. We could be taking the easy option, evading our responsibilities, or avoiding the necessity of making heart connections with others.

And we can find many, many things that can provide distraction or escapism within the walls of our rooms. (The World Wide Web is our oyster in this respect.) But here, in this context, let our room be a metaphor for a sanctuary, for a place where we can enjoy our own company, discover what's truly important to us and where we can train in the capacity to be alone.

So here, in our room, we can turn off the phone and computer. One of the first things I do when I go on retreat is remove my wallet and my watch, and place all my loose change and house keys in a drawer of the room or dormitory in which I'm staying. But we don't need to wait until we're on retreat to unburden ourselves. Alone in our room, we can also just let go of all those social expectations. We can remove the masks we're forced to adopt, masks we can't help but identify with sometimes, but which we know to be far less than the true representations of who we really are. In the essay on 'Self-Reliance' to which I've already referred, Emerson writes of these social masks, including:

> the forced smile which we put on in company where
> we do not feel at ease in answer to conversation which
> does not interest us. The muscles, not spontaneously
> moved, but moved by a low usurping wilfulness,
> grow tight about the outline of the face with the most
> disagreeable sensation.[29]

In the privacy of our room, we can relax those muscles. What a relief. We can let go. We can let go of the need to be gregarious – or even interesting. (There is an enormous, unseen pressure, externally and internally, to be interesting to others.) The more extrovert qualities are the ones more socially valued, but traits such as quietness and reflectiveness can be qualities in their own right. Again, shyness is not normally seen as a virtue, but in the

East it's often seen as quite an attractive quality to possess. Here in our room, we can be ourselves. We can relax. We can remind ourselves there is no shame in foregoing the party for the quieter pleasures of life that we can enjoy on our own.

And for a while we can just resist the desire to launch ourselves into a phone conversation or a newspaper – and just sit with boredom or loneliness, or even a slight sense of depression. Our lives are so full, so crammed with input and activity, that it can take quite a while for us to digest all that input, to clear a bit of space and light in that dark clutter of images, sounds, and half-remembered conversations. It's enough to just sit in our room, looking out of the window perhaps, or listening to 'the gas-fire breathe'. And as we just sit there, we'll find that the feelings of boredom, loneliness, or depression may slowly recede, and we'll experience a positive emotional charge as our eyes alight on the spine of a particular book, a poster or photograph on our wall, a particular object or ornament that means something to us. We will begin to notice what's important and meaningful to us here in our room, and what's superfluous, what doesn't need to be here. And if we sit, without distraction, for long enough, we may experience quite strong feelings of joy and contentment. There was a period, several years ago, when I spent quite a lot of my evenings just staring at the ceiling, allowing my thoughts to settle and my mind to clear. Those evenings were particularly pleasurable (although there was always that nagging voice that I should be *doing something useful*). The writer Franz Kafka put it beautifully:

> You do not need to leave your room. Remain sitting at your table and listen. Do not even listen, simply wait. Do not even wait, be quite still and solitary. The world will freely offer itself to you to be unmasked, it has no choice, it will roll in ecstasy at your feet.[30]

In our room we can resist the need to be useful. We can *be* rather than *do*. You could say that the yogi Milarepa's function in life was to expound the Dharma, the Buddha's teaching, in order that others might be liberated from their negative states of mind. This is true in a sense, but it wasn't as if Milarepa decided to assume a useful role in society. His teaching arose from a spontaneous outpouring of joy, love, and gratitude. He was expressing his true nature. He couldn't *but* sing the Dharma. The capacity to be alone involves discovering that spontaneous delight in just being ourselves. As Sangharakshita says:

> Our human existence is much more significant than we usually like to think. We can have no higher purpose than being ourselves. The only step worth taking from where we find ourselves as human beings is to evolve into Buddhas. We are not here to be useful. We don't have to justify our human status by engaging in some useful occupation. Of course there is nothing wrong with useful occupation, but we should beware of any idea that our purpose on this earth is to fill up our time with useful activities.[31]

Here in our room we can allow ourselves to be thoroughly useless. We can, for example, begin to rediscover our creativity. We can dust off the oboe that has been languishing under the bed for years. We can get out the watercolours, open the writing pad. I remember one friend suggesting to me that another mutual friend should give up playing the piano. 'What's the point? He's not going to be a Mozart.' Which significantly missed the point. By the same argument, we should only sing in the bath if we have a voice like Edith Piaf. In adult life, we can get oddly precious about our creative pursuits. They may mysteriously become such a source of pain or confusion that we feel we should put

45

them aside. But, when we were children, our drawing or writing was just an unselfconscious expression of who we were, a way of understanding ourselves and our world in an enjoyable way. When I was angry, I wrote funny little stories or drew cartoon figures with crayons, and the anger tended to vanish. I drew and wrote and made things because it would have just seemed weird not to. When we become adults we begin to ask ourselves difficult questions regarding our creativity: 'Is this good enough? Does this have any artistic merit whatsoever? Is this commercially viable? Why do I identify with this so much? Do I really have time for this? Is this as good as Betty's?' And, of course: 'Is this *useful*?' But we need to cultivate activities that we love, not necessarily for their utility. Here, in our room, we can do that without the necessity of knowing whether other people will approve of, applaud, or purchase what we are doing, singing, or producing.

It might seem that it's far easier to train in the capacity to be alone, easier to be useless and truly self-contained, when on retreat. Whether on a solitary retreat or on a retreat with others, many of our normal, daily distractions are no longer present. But I think we can fall prey to a misconception that the *real* work of the Buddhist life is done on retreat. Retreats can refresh our practice and help us connect with a sense of inspiration or vision. As we'll see in the next chapter, they can be particularly effective in helping us deal with entrenched habit. For some of us, retreat conditions provide a great opportunity to really make significant changes, and every Buddhist should try and get on retreat regularly. But it could be argued that the *real* work of the Buddhist life is done in our daily lives at home. Many of us are unable to get on retreat very often. We may be unable to afford it. We may have family commitments that mean it's very difficult to get away. So, for some of us, it may be family life that provides the crucible in which we're forced to dig further and discover deeper levels of patience and generosity in our hearts. It may be our experience in the workplace that forces us to develop a nourishing mindfulness practice without which our day might become a round of confusion, frustration, and pain. A sustaining sense of uselessness might be more firmly embedded in our lives if we can forge some time for harmonica practice in our room every night, while still holding down a demanding job in the Civil Service. For some of us, training in the capacity to be alone (whether we actually live alone or live with others) won't take place so much on solitary retreat as in the privacy of our own room. And because it has to be fought for more fiercely at home, our solitude might be more highly prized and our capacity to be alone take deeper root.

I know for a fact that there are many people out there, living alone in houses, flats, and apartments in the city, who don't get on retreat very often but who are highly spiritually developed. I know of prisoners who have beaten enormous odds to make significant changes to their lives, despite (one might even say because of) spending considerable time alone in their prison cells. The common factor among such people is the hard-won ability, in the midst of a busy or regimented life, to discipline oneself; to set up regular practices of meditation, reflection, or just doing nothing; to lock the doors of one's room for a set period. The examples of such people remind us that our room is not just a place where we perform the occasional holding operation until the *real* work on retreat begins. Our room can be a genuine sanctuary of retreat. Here we can gradually transform our life. In our room, for example, we can cultivate an effective practice of reflection during which we can let go of our habitual, haphazard ways of thinking. We can take a topic, or a theme, or a bit of text, and reflect purposefully on it, allowing our mind the space to really get to grips with it, and delight in it. Here in our room, we can make some regular time for ourselves to study the Buddha's teaching. These days we have access to a huge range of Buddhist texts, commentaries, and introductions, the vast majority of which was unavailable to previous generations. Here in my room, for example, I have the truly mind-blowing opportunity of communicating with the Enlightened mind of Milarepa. I have excellent translations, in English, of his songs and his life. Not only that. I have access to seminars and texts by my teacher that translate Milarepa's vision into a language with which I, as a Westerner, can very easily engage (Sangharakshita's commentary on some of Milarepa's songs, *The Yogi's Joy*, is the main text I've drawn upon for this book).

Just as amazingly, on the shelves and racks of our room, we have access to the work of some of the greatest writers, composers, and artists who have ever lived. How incredible that we can communicate with such minds in their absence, sometimes centuries after their deaths! One of the emphases of the Buddhist movement to which I belong is the importance of the arts. If we are to effectively engage with Buddhism, we need to discover images, stories, and music that help us connect, in a heartfelt way, with its practices and rituals. For some, the more traditional images and myths of Buddhism fulfil this function. For example, many of my friends really respond to the rich and colourful world of Tibetan Buddhism. For others, the need to make links with our own culture is more pressing. We need to build bridges between the Dharma and the poetry, music, and painting that we've grown up with and that speaks to us deeply. After all, the Buddha said that the Dharma should be preached in one's own dialect.

One of the main preoccupations of my own Buddhist life, and perhaps it's because I'm rather *wilfully* Western in my tastes, is to forge genuine connections between the Buddha's teaching, and the drama, theatre, and novels about which I'm passionate. (Perhaps you will have guessed at such a preoccupation from the style of this book!) I studied drama and English literature at university, but there wasn't enough for me there to base a life upon. I knew, when I discovered Buddhism, that this was where the truth lay. Yet I experienced the painful paradox that it was often the images, stories, and myths of Western literature that engaged me emotionally. Many of us, I know, experience a similar painful paradox. Here, in our room, we can begin to make those connections between the Dharma, and the music, art, and literature that fire our imaginations.

We can't get very far in the Buddhist life without connecting with a sense of pleasure and enjoyment. If we do begin to let go of the habitual cravings that have kept us tied to samsara, something must take the place of those desires – sources of enjoyment that can direct our emotions in the directions of Buddhist values. Which is certainly not to say that all we read or listen to should be sweetness and light. Part of our task is to understand pain, loneliness, and the darker side of our emotional lives. As we sit in our room, we can access an enormous source of pleasure by listening to music, reading, or looking at images that engage the heart. If such an engagement is more than just escapism, we'll come to realize that we're *not* alone here in our room. There's a communication going on. We'll begin to realize too that our feeling of essential aloneness is a shared human condition. Paradoxically, in that realization lies a true sense of connection with others. The best art takes us beyond the ego. The best art leads us to contemplate the feelings of others, to sympathize. It is that sympathy that enables us to break through the barriers of our own sense of separation and to realize how connected we really are.

So let's take time to select a book from our shelf – a volume of Emily Dickinson's poetry. Emily Dickinson was born in the conservative town of Amherst in New England in 1886. She always seems to have been quite sensitive, but was certainly not without a sense of humour and, like all the girls of the town, enjoyed a varied social life. But, as she grew older, she began to spend more and more time in her room in the homestead she shared with members of her family. Eventually she became a virtual recluse. In this room, over the years, she produced about 1,800 poems, only a dozen or so of which were published in her lifetime. Now, about a century after her death, she's recognized as a truly major poet.

Dickinson wasn't entirely reclusive. She baked, cooked, gardened, and looked after members of her family. She was shy of company but, now and then, would welcome the occasional visitor. Although she wasn't uninterested in the local gossip, the matters that really concerned her were the eternal and timeless ones:

> The only news I know
> Is bulletins all Day
> From Immortality[32]

Alone in her room, she perfected the verses that touched on the grand themes – loneliness, death, ecstasy . . . Not conventionally religious, her verses speak of a spirituality that celebrates the integrity and self-sufficiency of the individual soul, a kind of extreme spiritual individualism (which admittedly doesn't square with Buddhism). Her poems can initially seem quite difficult to understand with their strange syntax and unusual metaphors but, if we spend time with them, they can yield all kinds of insight and riches:

> Down Time's quaint stream
> Without an oar
> We are enforced to sail
> Our Port a secret
> Our Perchance a Gale
> What Skipper would
> Incur the Risk
> What Buccaneer would ride
> Without a surety from the Wind
> Or schedule of the Tide –[33]

What seafarer would set sail without knowing where he was going, without knowing the tides, with no idea of what kind of weather was in store? Yet this is the journey of our lives, heartbreaking in its haphazardness. In verses like these, Emily Dickinson encapsulates a fear we normally are only semi-aware of, and rarely articulate. The articulation of that fear makes us bigger as human beings, less lonely, aware that we are all in that very same boat. Emily Dickinson never embarked on a great journey across land or sea. She never felt the need to travel. Her verses, written in this one small room, explored her own vast, inner landscape – and they help us to explore our own. When we read a poet like Emily Dickinson, we have a confidence that our room can encapsulate eternity, that there is a great value in the capacity to be alone. In our room we can meet with the truth:

> Often in reading the poetry of Emily Dickinson we
> have the sense that her upstairs room had no ceiling,
> that the house itself had no roof but was open to the
> sky, that house and garden lay on a cosmic frontier.
> All time and space expand around her. Her basket, she
> said, held firmaments.[34]

Renunciation

In violently locking the door of his room, we could say that Philip Larkin was practising renunciation. Renunciation is very much part of the Buddhist life, and training in the capacity to be alone involves its effective and consistent practice. For many of us, however, the word 'renunciation' might seem problematic and unattractive. On the face of it, it seems life-denying, conjuring up images of a kind of grim-lipped, wilful negation. But the word and the practice might seem more appealing if we remind ourselves that renunciation is essentially the practice of removing the obstacles to our ecstasy. The fact that real happiness and freedom rely on subtraction and renunciation seems counter-intuitive. As we've seen, the instinctive response to feelings of emptiness and loneliness is to fill the void, to accumulate. In Roger Lewis' *The Life and Death of Peter Sellers* – a massive, opinionated, gloriously written, and compelling biography – the author reveals the extent to which this hugely talented and ultimately tragic man sought to alleviate his loneliness and sense of hollowness through accumulation, not just of people – though plenty of wives, lovers, and friends came and went – but of an astonishing array of objects, cameras, gadgets, houses, cars, toys . . .

> He collected toy railways, hi-fi hardware, anything
> clockwork or robotic. Covetous and acquisitive,
> he could always then give his playthings away or
> abandon them the moment they started to bore him.
> Bit players often tended to inherit his bits. Vacuum
> cleaners, obsolete tape recorders, lenses, a mechanical
> elephant, archery targets, a trampoline . . .[35]

Yet none of this brought him any happiness and, towards the end of his life, such was his fear and loneliness that he was sometimes unable to sleep without somebody holding his hand. His story is so fascinating because we recognize ourselves in it. Sellers was an extreme example of our tendency to run from loneliness and emptiness by way of acquisition. And reading the biography, I had a strong sense of how the need to accumulate and acquire people and things snowballs. It's as if acquisition necessitates more acquisition. In one of his seminars on Milarepa, Sangharakshita tells the salutary story of the monk whose guru left him to meditate. The disciple in question occasionally washed his loincloth and hung it out to dry, but he noticed that, when he did this, a rat would tend to nibble it. So the villagers brought him a cat to keep the rats at bay. The cat, of course, needed milk, which the villagers again provided, but after a while they suggested it might be easier if they just gave the disciple a cow that he could milk himself. So the monk milked the cow every day in order to acquire the milk to feed his cat to keep the rats which were nibbling his loincloth at bay. But he found he was spending a lot of his meditation time cutting grass for the cow so he asked somebody to cut the grass for him. Eventually this man had to be paid so the monk suggested the grass-cutter sell some of the milk the cow produced. More and more people began to buy the milk and soon a thriving business started. The villagers suggested it would be much easier if the monk married a woman who could manage the thriving business leaving the monk time to meditate . . . The upshot of the story is that the guru returned to find the monk married with a house, a herd of cows, servants, children, and a thriving dairy farm. Some of us might find some unsettling associations with our computers. (See also the Tootsi Frootsie ice-cream sequence in the Marx Brothers film *A Day at the Races*.)

So much of our happiness seems to rely on our myriad attachments and accumulations and acquisitions. Yet, as Stephen Batchelor puts it in *Alone with Others*:

> however hard we try, we will never succeed in filling
> an inner emptiness from the outside; it can only be
> filled from within. A lack of being remains unaffected
> by a plenitude of having.[36]

The Buddhist practice of renunciation challenges us to take the risk of subtracting rather than accumulating, not to immediately reach out to the world from a sense of loneliness or emptiness but to sit with the tension and be with ourselves more authentically.

The practice of renunciation challenges us to gradually let go of those addictions that deflect us from ourselves and our capacity to be alone without distraction.

And, if that still sounds too grim or difficult, we could reflect that, very often, the more we have, the less we *value* what we have. The writer Anthony de Mello suggests that most people

> have lost their capacity for enjoyment. I really believe that most people in affluent countries have lost that capacity. They've got to have more and more expensive gadgets; they can't enjoy the simple things of life.[37]

Renunciation involves simplifying our lives but, in the practice of simplicity, we can develop a greater appreciation and enjoyment of those things we do have. The art critic Robert Hughes made the very striking comment that we encounter more images in a day than somebody in the Middle Ages would have encountered in a lifetime. One can imagine how much the beautiful images and murals in a cathedral were prized by our distant ancestors. How wonderful it would be to prize images in that way.

We could reflect too that renunciation is essentially about giving up lesser pleasures for higher ones. It's as if we constantly settle for second best. Milarepa is joyful not *despite* having nothing but *because* he has nothing. The more he gives up, the happier he becomes. When a thief visited his cave one night, Milarepa called out, 'I don't think you'll be able to find anything there in the dark. I've never found anything even in daylight.' Renunciation may seem a difficult practice at first but, if we're practising it effectively, ultimately it will open up into joy. We've talked of faith and confidence arising from an awareness of duhkha. After faith, on the spiral path of positive nidanas or links, comes joy. As a result of our ongoing confidence in the Dharma comes a real relishing of it. We begin to delight in the Buddha's teaching. In terms of this book, based on our confidence in our ability to be alone without distraction, emerges a real joy in that solitude, in being less *encumbered*, in that more authentic way of being. This joy is something that can really sustain us in our spiritual lives:

> Only joy will keep us going in the spiritual life. You can only practise the Dharma if you have the energy, the spark, the zest for it. You need to be able to relish it for what it is – a feast for the famished heart and mind. If you do not love the Dharma passionately, even if you are a doctrine follower, you cannot live the life of renunciation authentically. It may take some effort before you enjoy your Dharma life, but enjoyment has to be on the agenda somewhere.[38]

Part of this sense of joy comes from a more outward-looking and empathetic attitude to life. We may lock the door of our room to get away from empty social obligations or idle conversation but, paradoxically, as we practise renunciation, as we let go of all our neurotic comforts and reassurances, we begin to more effectively connect with the world, even in our solitude. After all, what does Buddhism ask us to renounce? The habitual attachments and acquisitions that are self-centred and aren't doing us much good, those things we cling to in order to bolster the ego. As we've seen, it's ego-centredness that is the cause of our loneliness, our painful sense of separation. As we gradually and kindly transform all that energy that habitually goes into the overeating, the porn, the gadgets, the thousand small pleasures that we reach out for to dull the sting of our aloneness, we will necessarily become less self-centred, more aware of others, more inclined to be kind and generous. And more joyful. Joy will arise too as we let go of unhelpful patterns of thought. Such thought patterns are often even more difficult to renounce than physical acquisitions, as the Buddhist nun Tenzin Palmo comments:

> Genuine renunciation is giving up our fond thoughts, all our delight in memories, hopes and daydreams, our mental chatter. To renounce that, and stay naked in the present, that is renunciation . . .[39]

Meditation

One of the most effective ways of dealing with unhelpful patterns of thought is through meditation. When we meditate, we are training in the capacity to be alone. Although there is much to be gained from meditating in groups, even if we're meditating with others, we are essentially alone with our own minds. When we meditate we are trying to be more naked and authentic, attempting to see what lies behind this huge proliferation of thought. Just as, in our daily lives, we search for comforts and reassurances, people and objects, to distract ourselves from our essential aloneness, so in our mental lives we throw up all kinds of thoughts, chatter, and ruminations that deflect us from a more direct experience of our minds. We tend to identify closely with these thoughts and this chatter, but our thought patterns are ephemeral, and part of the work of meditation is to realize this, not to identify with thoughts, but to let them come and go like clouds in the sky. We have identified with some of these thought patterns so closely since childhood that they seem essentially part of who we are. Yet with patient and kindly practice, even these deep-rooted thoughts can be seen to be just passing through. With practice too, we realize to what extent we gain comfort from identifying with certain thought patterns, even particularly negative ones. There can be something quite reassuring about continually telling ourselves that we are not worth very much, that we're going to fail again, that we're not up to the mark.

Some of us can be afraid of what we might find when we meditate. An obstacle to going deeper in meditation is the fear, not always conscious, that, if we let go of all our habitual thoughts and pleasant, comforting fantasies, we might discover something basically nasty. We have had enough glimpses of our own negativity, and we know enough world history, to be easily persuaded that the human mind is essentially evil. It's certainly true that, if we have an effective meditation practice, we will have to face the darker side of our nature. We should be prepared for the often humiliating experience of discovering within our mind deep hatred, chronic anxiety, neurotic yearning . . . This is one of the reasons we don't practise in isolation. To deal with some of the things the mind throws up, friendship and guidance are necessary. But the more effective our meditation practice becomes, the more we learn to essentially trust our mind. We begin to have more and more faith in the deeper foundation of awareness, strength, and joy that characterises the mind in its true and naked state. As we train in the capacity to be alone, and as our meditation practice becomes more effective, we begin to glimpse and trust the essential beauty of our wild, unbounded mind.

In her handbook for writers, *Wild Mind*, Natalie Goldberg, also a practising Buddhist, introduces her advice and exercises by saying that life is not orderly, and that it defies our attempts to control it:

> In summer, we work hard to make a tidy garden, bordered by pansies with rows or clumps of columbine, petunias, bleeding-hearts. Then we find ourselves longing for the forest, where everything has the appearance of disorder, yet we feel peaceful there.

Writing, like Zen practice, she suggests, attempts to access the natural, wild state of the mind:

> The mind is raw, full of energy, alive and hungry. It
> does not think in the way we were brought up to think
> – well mannered, congenial.[40]

When we meditate we begin to become more acquainted with this wild mind. Perhaps the reason for so much of our unhappiness and boredom is that our mind can seem enclosed and contained by the familiar privet, columbine, and petunias that we've been cultivating and admiring for years. Our neat rows of pansies can seem the bounds of the known universe. Yet something in us yearns for the forest, for the more elemental nature of our mind. In meditation, we can begin to leave the familiarity of suburbia and enter the forest. There we will encounter darkness and fear, but we will also learn to trust that underlying strength and positivity to which I've referred. And we will have access to deeper and deeper levels of energy. In terms of the spiral path of positive links, dependent on joy arises bliss or rapture, a state of radiant energy. In Buddhist iconography there are many figures blazing with light and energy. We're iconographically unused to such figures, and to us they may appear demonic – which they're not. My early model for spirituality was the Jesus pictured in my children's Bible. He was pale and wan and may have had wisdom and kindness, but he seemed to have very little energy. In Buddhism, it is a sublime state of energy that, along with compassion and wisdom, is said to characterize the Enlightened mind.

I won't enumerate the subsequent steps of the spiral path of positive nidanas. It's enough to say that they constitute a series of cumulative and ever more positive states of mind, states of mind into which the previous state is integrated. So, for example, our physical rapture is contained and held in ever more deepening states of tranquillity and calm. And of course, even though an effective spiritual practice is characterized by such creative and spiral conditioning, our actual experience is not like climbing a spiral staircase. We don't leave duhkha behind after the first step. Experientially, the spiritual life might seem more like a game of snakes and ladders. In our meditation practice, for example, we may be bewildered that, after a sit characterized by a profound sense of calm and bliss, we experience, in our next meditation, some very painful childhood memories. But this may well have happened because our mind was ready to receive such pain, because the positive states of mind were able to contain the difficult memories. Similarly, after a period in our Buddhist life where we feel engaged, happy, and generous, we may suddenly feel as if we're falling apart. Again, this may be the inevitable consequence of *positive* states of mind, rather than the opposite. The Buddhist life never follows a neat trajectory. However, underneath the highs and lows, we can trust that an *effective* Buddhist practice is characterized by this underlying spiral and cumulative conditioning. If we don't react to the inevitable pain and difficulties that our spiritual practice throws up in the old, habitual, cyclic way, then our progress will *generally* follow the direction of up and up – rather than round and round. And if our spiritual practice is effective, then we will inevitably become more altruistic. In terms of an effective meditation practice, we'll experience again this seeming paradox: that the more we sit alone on our meditation cushions, experiencing the wild, elemental spaciousness of our own mind, the more aware we will be of others, the more we will want to help others overcome their painful sense of isolation.

Milarepa

The main role model for a Buddhist is, of course, the Buddha himself. But other figures in Buddhist myth and history provide a model, their lives seeming to offer an archetypal significance. This is true of Milarepa, who was a great sinner who became a great saint, and whose life was marked by intense suffering – and intense joy. Because his story is a story of such extremes, it more clearly shows the nature and trajectory of the Buddhist life. In terms of this book, Milarepa's life provides us with a vivid model in our investigation of the themes of solitude, loneliness, and the capacity to be alone.

Milarepa's father died when Milarepa was still a boy, and the family's inheritance was embezzled by a wicked aunt and uncle, forcing Milarepa, his sister, and his mother into a life of hardship and poverty. His mother harboured a fierce hatred in her heart and eventually persuaded her son to exact revenge. So Milarepa learnt sorcery and black magic and eventually used his powers to destroy many of his enemies. In the mother's hatred and shrewdness, and in Milarepa's desire to please his mother, and subsequent acts of vengeance, we can observe the reactive, cyclic, and samsaric mind at its most intense. In a sense, it's reassuring to us that Milarepa performed some terrible atrocities. As with other tales of men and women who've performed terrible crimes but have finally discovered spiritual redemption, we say to ourselves: 'If he could do all that and still become Enlightened, then there's hope for me yet . . .'

Milarepa soon became aware of the moral consequences of his crimes, and what was in store for him if he didn't somehow make amends and transform his life. So he sought out a teacher, the eccentric Marpa, who, aware of the extent of the young man's bad karma, put Milarepa through some terrible ordeals. He demanded that Milarepa build a stone tower with his own hands, but when Milarepa had finished the task, Marpa wasn't satisfied and the young man had to start all over again. And then again. And again. As soon as one tower was finished, Marpa would decide that it was in the wrong place, or it was the wrong shape, or it was the wrong size. Milarepa was brought to the verge of madness and suicide. His sense of pain and isolation was almost too much to bear. Our sense of loneliness and isolation is often at its most acute when we clearly realize the extent and consequences of some of our shameful actions, but either can't, or won't, run from the realization. Marpa's wife tried to comfort Milarepa, but he had nowhere to run to. He knew that he couldn't give in, that his bad karma had to be worked through. He had to sit with the agony of shame and regret, endure his loneliness and sense of painful isolation. But gradually the pain seasoned him and Milarepa discovered a huge faith and confidence in Marpa, who finally gave him initiations into the Buddha's teaching.

Karmically purified, Milarepa practised meditation and renunciation, determined to become Enlightened. During those years of struggle, Milarepa occasionally still experienced loneliness and isolation. Meditating on his own in the mountains, he missed his teacher. He missed his Buddhist companions and the ordinary human contact and warmth they provided. And, on one occasion, going in search of his family, he had a terrible shock. Returning to his home village, he found the old field his family had cultivated overgrown with weeds. The house in which he'd lived with his mother and sister was deserted and in a state of ruin. Rats and mice were everywhere. Then . . .

> I entered the main room. The ruins of the hearth
> mingling with dirt formed a heap where weeds
> grew and flourished. There were many bleached and
> crumbled bones. I realized that these were the bones
> of my mother. At the memory of her, I choked with
> emotion, and overcome with grief, I nearly fainted.[41]

Milarepa sat on the bones of his mother and there, in the ruined house, meditated and dedicated himself even more intensely to the pursuit of Enlightenment. Can there be a more striking image of loneliness than this picture of the grief-stricken son meditating on the bones of his mother, the mother whom he had loved so intensely and for whom he had committed such terrible crimes?

Gradually, as Milarepa got deeper into his practice, his sense of aloneness became bracing rather than isolating. He began to relish this solitary life, this life of pure simplicity. He began to exemplify the qualities on the spiral path that we've been looking at – the awareness of duhkha, the sense of faith and confidence, the supreme joy in the spiritual life, the radiant energy . . . And, eventually, as he totally left behind the cyclic, samsaric conditioning and accumulated more and more positive emotion, he finally broke through into Buddhahood.

Milarepa is a great exemplification of the capacity to be alone and of trusting one's inner resources. Again and again he sings of the delights of meditation, of his delight in this simple life of pure renunciation. His aloneness is a source of joy. He has renounced companions and property and is blissfully happy. He feels completely in tune with his environment and with the creatures who inhabit it. He has also renounced the sense of separate selfhood, his ego, and thus can no longer feel loneliness:

> If your experience of 'yourself' is not separateness but
> the blissful void, you have transcended the duality of
> self and other that is the ultimate basis for loneliness.
> You are no longer an ego and therefore no longer
> distinct from other egos. How can you feel lonely if you
> don't experience the ultimate reality of yourself – even
> when absolutely alone – as separate from others?[42]

And this brings us to one of the final reasons why Milarepa's life serves as an important model for Buddhists. In the state of egolessness that Milarepa's solitude and practice has brought him to, he is utterly other-regarding. Milarepa's life shows that the life of solitude is not necessarily the life of selfishness. Milarepa, in his supreme kindness and wisdom, always finds the appropriate words and teachings for the disciples, shepherds, hunters, scholars, and even demons who visit his cave. In his total devotion to his teacher, Marpa, and in his concern for his disciples, Milarepa sings of the delights of spiritual friendship. Milarepa celebrates altruism in his songs. Compassion, generosity, and wisdom are not grim duties but spontaneous, delightful, and natural expressions of egolessness. Milarepa demonstrates that the life of altruism is the life of joy. A thousand years after his death, he is still an example and inspiration to Buddhist practitioners.

Of course, we don't have to follow Milarepa's example literally, and find ourselves an isolated cave. I hope this chapter has shown that, with a bit of effort, solitude can be enjoyed in the city, in our room, in the situations in which we find ourselves. Yet there is something about wild places, about dwelling alone in nature, that calls to us. Reading Milarepa's songs or his life story, we feel drawn to the eagles, the streams, the snow, the hail, the fish, the mountains, the cliffs, the thunder . . . The solitude . . . Perhaps, then, it's time to look up our bus and train timetables, pack our rucksack and unlock the door of our room. Perhaps it's time to venture outside, into the wilds.

4

Solitude

Into the Wilds

I went to the woods because I wished to live deliberately,
to front only the essential facts of life, and see if I could
not learn what it had to teach, and not, when I came to die,
discover that I had not lived.

Henry David Thoreau,
Walden; or, Life in the Woods[43]

'Sermons in stones . . .'

Why, since the time of the Buddha, have Buddhist practitioners been encouraged to undergo periods of solitude in wild and isolated places? If, as I've argued, we can effectively train in the capacity to be alone in our own room, why then do we need to venture out into nature at all?

In the last chapter I quoted from Natalie Goldberg's book, *Wild Mind*:

> The mind is raw, full of energy, alive and hungry. It
> does not think in the way we were brought up to think
> – well mannered, congenial.[44]

One of the aims of Buddhist practice is to delve below the superficial, repetitive, and obsessive nature of the mundane

65

mind, and to access something more elemental and authentic. And when we spend time in wild places we're constantly offered reminders of, and metaphors for, the more fundamentally wild, energetic, and dynamic nature of the mind. There's something about looking up at a range of mountains, for example, that speaks to us of our infinite potential. When we gaze over a loch, we can be reminded of the vast pools of energy that lie below the surface of our normally choked and cluttered minds. Walking by a turbulent sea, we're offered a potent metaphor for the dynamic and ever-changing nature of consciousness itself. And those rows of sunbathers, lining the beach and staring up into the sky, are partly there (whether they're aware of it or not) to experience echoes of the fundamentally open and spacious nature of their mind, to remind themselves that their day-to-day experience of their constricted and cramped consciousness is not the whole story. Ultimately, a shopping mall and a wild wood partake of the same reality. But walking through a wild wood, on our own, offers us more clues to the nature of that reality than an afternoon spent in a cluttered shopping mall.

In Shakespeare's *As You Like It*, the usurped Duke Senior and his followers are forced to flee from the court and live in the woods. Here, the duke rouses his dejected courtiers, praising life in the woods over the artificial life of the court, happily declaring that the wind and the elements are 'counsellors that feelingly persuade me what I am'. In exile from the 'painted pomp' of court life, they all may

> Find tongues in trees, books in the running brooks,
> Sermons in stones, and good in everything.[45]

So one of the advantages of going on a solitary retreat is that, if we're open and receptive, the natural environment can teach us about ourselves and about the nature of our minds. We can learn a lot, for example, from the animals we come across on our walks. I don't mean this in any sentimental or anthropomorphic way: despite much argument to the contrary, human beings are brainier than dolphins. But the cry of a seagull can plaintively speak to us of our own aloneness, its flight across the sky, of our own deep yearning for freedom. Observing the unhurried grace and elegance of a swan, we can suddenly become aware of our own unnecessary anxiety and impatience, and can more easily let it all go. Walking through a field, and coming across a lamb's corpse, we are powerfully reminded that death can come to us at any time. And what about that stag I suddenly stumbled upon, at the brow of a hill, during my last solitary retreat? The gaze it trained upon me before bounding off communicated something quite thrilling – although I'd be very hard pressed to explain what that 'something' was.

Sometimes we can speak of 'going into nature' as if the experience is predictable and uniform, as if we expect to hear the same sermon every time we get off the coach marked 'COUNTRYSIDE'. But, of course, there are as many sermons as there are stones, as many preachers as there are rivers, all with their own particular style and delivery. We might find a particular environment rousing and another calming. Some landscapes might fill our hearts with joy while others might not speak to us at all. And certain wild places we might find threatening, scary, or even depressing.

For many years, round about Christmas, I used to go on a month's solitary retreat to a friend's converted windmill in Norfolk. The countryside around the mill was flat, the skies vast, and I used to very much enjoy my undemanding walks in those sharp, clear winter mornings. From a vantage point on the roof of the mill, I could look out over the farms, fields, and villages, and count the handsome flint churches that dotted the landscape and seemed to offer some kind of spiritual reassurance.

As on any solitary retreat, I experienced difficult periods, but I remember those retreats as generally refreshing, stilling, and calming, the landscape speaking to me of my own potential for deep tranquillity and peace of mind. One year, I decided not to go back to the mill for my solitary retreat, but to rent a cottage in a fishing village on the Moray Coast, in north-east Scotland. It was a place where I used to holiday as a boy and I knew it to be a wild and beautiful place. On that particular retreat I encountered some very turbulent states of mind, including acute fear and anxiety. Although the weather was extremely stormy, I went for a walk every day, struggling along the rain-lashed beach, wrapped in jumpers and waterproofs. Some days, I'd take the cliff path and, as I watched the breakers rolling in from the North Sea and crashing on the rocks far below, these lines from the poet Gerald Manley Hopkins would often come to mind:

> O the mind, mind has mountains; cliffs of fall
> Frightful, sheer, no-man-fathomed . . .[46]

It's interesting to reflect why I chose to go to the fishing village that particular year, and not to the mill. I think I may have had a sense that turbulent states of mind were beginning to rise in my mind, and I wanted to be in a landscape that might reflect the turbulence. So, although this was not particularly conscious, I chose a place for my solitary retreat that I knew from my childhood to be wild and dramatic, somewhere that might speak to me of the wild and passionate forces in my own mind. But the landscape also had many happy memories for me, and those happy memories helped me to deal with, and contain, the difficult mental states that arose.

We could say, generally speaking, that the first stage of Buddhist practice is aimed at developing positive states of mind such as calm, tranquillity, loving-kindness, and concentration. On this basis, through reflection, meditation, or some other means, a

Buddhist then attempts to see through the limitations of the ego-bound consciousness, into the very truth of things. At some stages in our Buddhist career, especially in our first years of practice, we will concentrate more on developing calm and positive states of mind. At other stages in our career, the development of insight into reality may become more of a priority. And the experience of being alone in nature can really assist both of these stages. From the natural environment we can take what we might need to stimulate and encourage the process.

For a Buddhist, part of the importance of being alone in nature is that it helps us get in touch with this first stage of practice, helps us develop states of calm and tranquillity. Being on our own in the country can help us more readily let go of the preoccupations and anxieties that can consume us in the city. We can slow down. Being in an environment that is less cramped, less frantic, and more beautiful, we can more readily trust the elements of spaciousness, calm, and beauty in our own minds. Often, as we walk alone in nature, we can access what feels like a very basic sense of joy and pleasure, a joy that sustains and nourishes us as we meditate, study, or quietly get on with the daily activities of our solitary retreat. And all these positive states of mind can also be recollected and incorporated into our practice long after our retreat is over.

For the Romantic poet William Wordsworth the recollection of the emotions experienced in beautiful, natural environments was constant sustenance to his mind and to his poetry. He tells us that often, 'in lonely rooms and mid the din of towns and cities', such healing memories provided

> In hours of weariness, sensations sweet,
> Felt in the blood, and felt along the heart,
> And passing even into my purer mind
> With tranquil restoration . . .[47]

For Wordsworth, his experiences of being in nature, and the recollection of these experiences, connected him to a principle of serenity, joy, and harmony, a spirit that he felt underlay and pervaded all existence. Being in contact with this spirit enabled the poet to hear, and to communicate, what he called 'the still, sad music of humanity'[48] and 'to see into the life of things'.[49] Wordsworth's poem 'Daffodils' has been virtually ruined for generations of British schoolchildren, who have had to learn it by heart and recite it in front of the class. It has become stale with overfamiliarity, which is a pity because, in this little poem, it's almost as if we're presented with Wordsworth's manifesto for living. Here we have the poet wandering alone in nature, 'lonely as a cloud', but becalmed and saved from isolation by the sight of thousands of wild daffodils. As he gazes at the flowers, he sees into the harmonious, joyful spirit that connects man and environment, and his loneliness is forgotten. The poem ends with the memory of the encounter providing the poet with sustenance in solitude, his heart once again dancing with the wild daffodils.

Wordsworth's emphasis was on the calming, joyful, and restorative aspects of contact with nature. But there is another aspect to the Romantic response to nature, and it's an aspect that is also useful to a Buddhist practitioner. This response is more to do with the awe-inspiring, the sublime, the dreadful, the terrifying . . . In Coleridge's 'Rime of the Ancient Mariner', a sailor brings a curse upon himself, his ship, and his shipmates when he kills an albatross. The sea and sky offer no comfort, no sense of healing or 'tranquil restoration', to the besieged mariner as his companions die of thirst, and as he himself is plunged into a hellish, solitary, nightmare world:

> Alone, alone, all all alone
> Alone on the wide wide Sea;
> And Christ would take no pity on
> My soul in agony.

The many men so beautiful,
And they all dead did lie!
And a million, million slimy things
Liv'd on – and so did I!

I look'd upon the rotting Sea,
And drew my eyes away;
I look'd upon the eldritch deck,
And there the dead men lay.

I look'd to Heaven, and tried to pray;
But or ever a prayer had gusht,
A wicked whisper came and made
My heart as dry as dust.[50]

This is a far cry from Wordsworth's meditative boatings on a calm lake. Wordsworth himself spoke of 'the sublime', that response to nature that inspires awe, but his own poetry prized harmony and tranquillity over those elements of fear and dread that came to be associated with the word. Edmund Burke, who was one of the first writers to attempt to define the sublime, associated it with a feeling of 'delightful horror, a sort of tranquillity tinged with terror'.[51] And in their poems and paintings, we see many Romantic poets and artists becoming more and more fascinated with shipwrecks, storms, vast mountain ranges, volcanic eruptions, typhoons, avalanches . . . When we effectively respond to the sublime, whether present in an actual landscape, or represented in a work of art, we experience a fear and an awe in the face of the vastness, the raw and elemental power, the indifference of nature. Such terrible power threatens to overwhelm the small, fragile self. Yet it is a 'delightful' fear because there is also in us that which aspires to the egoless and selfless, which invites the dissolution of the self, and so responds to the vastness and power of these subjects.

So time spent on a solitary retreat can be restorative, but it can also be challenging. If you are in sufficiently calm and positive states of mind, you might introduce elements of such challenge into your retreat. You might consciously decide to spend time in a landscape or environment that evokes for you this sense of the sublime, this 'tranquillity tinged with terror'. In this way you might reflect on how little control your small self can exert over life in general; how, in order to progress, you must rather let go into the dynamic and energetic play of reality. On your walks, rather than take a little detour to avoid the corpse of the lamb, you can allow the sight to remind you of your own dissolution and death. You can embrace your fear.

Ultimately, a Buddhist is attempting to go beyond fear entirely. But, as we shall soon see, to go beyond fear, you need to face up to it. Such an experience can be delightful, as well as uncomfortable, as you begin to have more and more of a sense of the potency and energy that your habitual anxiety keeps in check. On a solitary retreat, you should first attempt to become acquainted with the restorative angel, the spirit who reintroduces you to a sense of harmony, calm, and connectedness. But, when you're ready, you might ask this angel to introduce you to the destructive angel, her more daunting and challenging sister, who will ask you to address both your fear and the entrenched habit that keeps that fear in place.

Habit

According to Buddhism, our loneliness and isolation stem from a belief in a fixed and unchanging self. Buddhist practice is aimed at going beyond this belief in a fixed self and moving towards egolessness, towards a state of mind in which we are at ease with the ever-changing, dynamic nature of reality. Such a state is embodied in the supremely spontaneous and joyful figure of Milarepa. As we've seen, in order to avoid experiencing loneliness, isolation, and suffering, our actions tend towards the habitual, the cyclic, the addictive, and the repetitive. Unfortunately, this behaviour only serves to reinforce our sense of this isolated and unchanging entity we call the self. Traditionally, this belief in a fixed and permanent self is one of the first fetters that needs to be broken before a Buddhist can reach the stage of spiritual development called Stream Entry. For a Stream Entrant, the spiritual momentum behind their practice means that Enlightenment is eventually assured. In a lecture entitled The Taste of Freedom, Sangharakshita translates this traditional fetter of fixed self-view in very basic, down-to-earth terms, as habit:

> The person we think of as George or Mary, and
> recognize as acting in a particular way, is simply a
> habit that a certain stream of consciousness has got
> into. But since it has got into it, it can get out of it. It
> is like a knot tied in a piece of string; it can be untied.
> Breaking the fetter of habit means, essentially, getting
> out of the habit of being a particular kind of person.[52]

In the last chapter, we explored many of the benefits of solitude and we saw how these benefits can be enjoyed by just spending time alone in our room. We saw that we don't necessarily have to disappear into the country to access the spiritual joys and challenges of solitude. Indeed, solitude's benefits might be more enduring if we have the self-discipline to regularly train in the capacity to be alone in our day-to-day lives. Yet it's also true that the process of training in the capacity to be alone can be considerably heightened and intensified if we spend time alone in nature. Doing this can also make the process much easier. Removing ourselves from our usual environment makes it easier, for example, to address our entrenched habits, as Anthony Storr points out in *Solitude*:

> Whether in young or old, changes of attitude are facilitated by solitude and often by change of environment as well. This is because habitual attitudes and behaviour often receive reinforcement from external circumstances.[53]

Storr gives the example of smoking – how the desire for a cigarette occurs according to particular cues at particular intervals in the day. So we might associate having a cigarette with sitting down at a familiar desk, or with specific times during working hours, or with reading the newspaper. But, in a place more unfamiliar to us, we tend not to do the same things at the same times, which is why many people find it easier to give up smoking on holiday. So, where our entrenched habits rely on external stimuli, the easiest way to challenge those habits is by simply removing the external stimuli. We subtract. We renounce. We remove ourselves from our normal environment. The regular visit to the pub on Thursday evenings is now no longer a possibility. We go somewhere where the books, computer, phone, car, favourite foods, television, iPod, and other entities that can habitually distract us from our deeper purpose are just not present. And, astonishingly, we usually survive. In fact, we often thrive. We realize that life without a BlackBerry is not only possible, but potentially liberating. We can gain confidence in the fact that we are not the objects and comforts we habitually rely upon. 'Simplify, simplify', railed Thoreau in *Walden*,[54] an account of his two years, from 1845 to 1847, spent in virtual seclusion in the woods of Massachusetts. In the previous chapter I said that our habitual reaction to loneliness and emptiness is to acquire, to accumulate, and that Buddhist practice tends to emphasize renunciation and subtraction – removing the obstacles to our ecstasy. A solitary retreat gives us a real chance to subtract and simplify, a process that is even more necessary for us acquisitive, twenty-first-century creatures than it was for Thoreau's contemporaries.

On solitary retreat, for example, we're able to reduce much of the input and information that habitually crowds in on our senses. What would Thoreau have made of our twenty-four-hour, rolling-news channels? He was scathing enough of his *own* contemporaries' addiction to news:

> After a night's sleep the news is as indispensable as the breakfast. 'Pray tell me anything new that has happened to a man anywhere on this globe', – and he reads it over his coffee and rolls, that a man has had his eyes gouged out this morning on the Wachito River; never dreaming the while that he lives in the dark unfathomed mammoth cave of this world, and has but the rudiment of an eye himself.[55]

It could be argued that we need to keep abreast of what's going on in the world. This may be true to a certain extent, but how much of the news or gossip that we take in is at all relevant twenty-four hours after we've heard it? Our addiction to news, information, and gossip is just another habit, often based on anxiety, or on a neurotic desire for sensation, or on the mistaken belief that, in acquiring news, we can somehow control events. One of the great benefits of a solitary retreat is the chance to renounce the news for a while. We have the opportunity, for example, to let go of the habit of reading the Sunday papers, those vast slabs of newsprint that, in a single issue, seem to contain more words than all of Dickens' novels put together, but, unlike Dickens' novels, leave us feeling concussed, depressed, and enervated.

Just as we're habituated to a world of information, we're also habituated to a world of noise. We can't travel a couple of metres in a lift without being subjected to 'soothing' music. The appreciation of silence can be another great benefit of going on solitary retreat. Our habitual desire for music or conversation means that we may find silence challenging at first, but we may also be surprised at how quickly silence can begin to feel nourishing and refreshing. For me, the enjoyment of silence is one of the great pleasures of going on a solitary retreat. Such silence is not just an absence. As we let go of our habitual tendency to crave noise, inner and outer, our minds can become calm and limpid. We find that true silence is vibrant and alive. The writer Sara Maitland wrote a whole book about silence and about her personal search for environments where the experience of silence is at its most profound and nourishing. Maitland is a Christian, and the following passage is couched in theistic terms, but I think we might easily translate what she says here into the kind of terms we've been using in this book. Silence, she seems to be saying, is not an absence, but comprises a vibrant sense of freedom that challenges our narrow, fixed self-view:

> In the desert I learned that silence is more for me
> than a context for prayer, or a way of creating more
> time (though those are important). It is, in itself, a
> form of freedom; it generates freedom, free choices,
> inner clarity, strength. A freedom from one's self and
> a freedom to be oneself. . . . I started to think that
> perhaps silence is God. Perhaps God is silence – the
> shining, spinning ring 'of pure and endless light'.[56]

A nourishing experience of silence relies on renouncing the habitual, and seemingly comforting, desire for background noise, conversation, and music. Such subtraction allows us to meet our mind in a deeper, more elemental way. In the same way, on solitary retreat, we can *live* in a more elemental way, by the subtraction of many of our habitual comforts. It's up to us how far we want to take this. Some friends, I know, don't like their solitary venues to be too uncomfortable. Others are happy with quite spartan accommodation. But deliberately pushing against the boundaries of our normal comfort zone can be refreshing and energizing. We are generally very well insulated these days against discomfort. With air conditioning or central heating, for example, we can pretty much control our immediate environment. Technology has freed us from many of the labour-intensive chores that were daily duties for our grandparents, even our parents. But what we gain from our labour-saving devices and habitual comforts can be offset by feeling, at times, less truly alive. Being on solitary retreat, alone in nature, we are more likely to get our hands dirty. We are more likely to come in contact with rock, peat, wood, rain, snow, wind, stone, water, fire. Rather than order our shopping online, we may have to walk a few miles, through hail, for a loaf. We may have to chop wood for a fire (a particular pleasure for me on one retreat I remember). Our sensual experience is often more immediate and less vicarious on a solitary retreat. Rather than watching a film of a storm, we might find ourselves in the middle of one. And stripped of certain habitual comforts, we may realize how little we can truly control the elements, our environment – even our lives in general. The weather may disrupt our plans. The vagaries of nature may mean we're caught in places or situations we'd rather not be. Some of my more adventurous friends have even found themselves sharing a living space with the local animal life. Yet, in letting go of habitual comforts, we can feel more present, more authentic, more rooted to the earth and to the life around us.

Another great benefit of being on solitary retreat is that we've removed ourselves from other people. In the penultimate chapter we'll be looking at how we need other people. Others can inspire, support, encourage, and love. Yet the company of others can also be one of the greatest distractions to leading a deeper, more meaningful life. Other people can reinforce the fixed self-view, the rigid, habitual behaviour that keeps us imprisoned. Sangharakshita says:

> It is not easy to get out of the habit of being the kind of person that we are. One of the reasons for this is other people. Not only have we ourselves got in the habit of being in a particular way, but other people have got into the habit of experiencing us as being in the habit of being in a particular way.[57]

On solitary retreat, we can let go of our roles, our habitual ways of being with others, which can be so constricting. We can stop playing up to others' perceptions of us. We can remove that fixed social mask that Emerson so disapproved of,

> the forced smile which we put on in company where we do not feel at ease in answer to conversation which does not interest us.[58]

I remember going for a walk on one solitary retreat and suddenly experiencing a sense of relief that I didn't have to worry about my appearance, that, in the great scheme of things, what I was wearing and how I physically appeared to others (particularly how my face appeared to others) didn't matter one jot. One of the reasons Siddhartha, the Buddha to be, left home and sought the truth alone in the forest was that, although he himself may have renounced his roles as warrior and prince, others would have continued to perceive him in this way. It was only in solitude, through being a non-person, that Siddhartha could finally understand who he really was, and in what his role really consisted. One of the happiest moments in the life of Charlie Brown, the cartoon creation of Charles Schulz, is when, at summer camp, he puts a bag over his head to hide a rash. The other kids, not realizing that this is Charlie, the perennial loser, begin to respect the mysterious kid, call him 'Mr Sack', and elect him camp president. Then he takes the bag off . . . I suspect that Charlie Brown may have had to spend a fair bit of time in solitude in later life.

On solitary retreat we leave behind others and many of our habitual distractions and comforts, but the one thing we can't leave behind is our own mind, with all its habitual patterns of thought. It comes with us. I had one friend, with whom I lived in a Buddhist community, who was always finding fault with aspects of our living situation. The community was never tidy enough, the bathroom never clean enough, the other community members always too messy or unmindful. On my friend's first solitary retreat he had a very hard time, at least initially. His first three days were spent organizing and reorganizing the simple solitary hut in which he was staying. He swept and cleaned and ushered out insects, but he just couldn't get the hut the way he wanted it. Finally the penny dropped. It wasn't the hut that was the problem but his own habitual and neurotic tendency to demand some kind of perfection of his living space. Similarly, on one retreat, I began to reflect on a schoolteacher I'd had, a stern brute of a man. These reflections began to shade into obsessive, hateful thoughts, and I berated him again and again for his cruelty and unfairness. Eventually though, I began to ask myself why I was obsessing about the teacher, and realized that I was projecting my own habitual (and current) tendency to violent self-criticism on to the memory of this man. On solitary retreat, removed from other people and our usual environment, we can become more aware that our difficulties do not always arise from external situations or other people, but from our own habitual tendencies towards hatred, desire, and anxiety. We can notice how such tendencies seek a hook to hang themselves upon, or an external object or person upon which to express themselves. And in cultivating that awareness, we allow ourselves the freedom to choose between acting in this fixed, repetitive, habitual way, and pursuing a more creative response.

If, on solitary retreat, you start to effectively chip away at such repetitive and seemingly fixed behaviour, you will find yourself naturally acting more spontaneously. Without other people's eyes upon you, and in letting go of rigid habits of mind, you might even find yourself singing and dancing. On a long solitary retreat on North Uist, I would often go for long walks during which I wouldn't pass a soul. I used to find myself singing (actually bawling at the top of my voice) ridiculous, improvised, comic songs. I could understand then the so-called 'madness' of some of those solitary hermits and could appreciate why Milarepa regularly burst into spontaneous outpourings of song! As social creatures we are habituated to behaviour that regularly inhibits our joy and spontaneity.

All habit of course is not negative or unhelpful, and all habit does not reinforce fixed self-view. As you *are* a creature of habit, one benefit of a solitary retreat might be the relative ease with which you may be able to create *positive* habits. And these you can take back with you to your workaday world. You might establish a regular meditation practice on solitary retreat, for example, that continues when you get home. On returning from a solitary retreat you may find that, to some extent, you've established positive habits of reflection and mindfulness that more readily undermine your negative patterns of thought and behaviour.

Fear

We incline so much towards habit because our habits offer us illusions of security and control. Our seemingly fixed and unchanging self needs that security and tends to embrace the known, the safe, and the comfortable. It tends to distrust new ways of doing things. Buddhism tells us that existence is an impermanent, dynamic interplay of ever-shifting conditions. Nothing is fixed, permanent, or assured. Aligning our small, fixed selves with repetition and habit, particularly regarding those things that give us pleasure, is an attempt to keep these truths at bay. We fear the insubstantial, impermanent nature of reality, upon which there is no secure ground to stand. We attempt to create little islands of permanence, stability, and substantiality; attempt to ignore the shifting sands beneath our feet. But a Buddhist life is one that is committed to going beyond habit and fixed self-view. This means that we are consciously moving towards the unknown, beyond what is comfortable, assured, and secure. And this, of course, can be frightening. So Buddhists inevitably invite fear into their lives. One situation in which we face such fear is on a solitary retreat, where our habitual distractions, comforts, and thoughts are less likely to offer a false security.

We spend a lot of our lives afraid. This fear is not fear that is being faced and challenged, but often a grumbling, semi-conscious anxiety. On solitary retreat particularly, I am aware of how, when I've solved one anxiety, my mind almost immediately latches on to something else to worry about. It seems that we're afraid to let go of anxiety because to let go of anxiety would be to relinquish control of our lives. And anxiety is about controlling and organizing the future. We cannot be anxious and truly present. And so we become defined by our anxieties, habituated to anxiety. Anxiety is so difficult to relinquish because it is who we seem to be. To stop being anxious would mean letting go of who we are, letting go of control, allowing the future to manifest without the interference of our little self's demands. Anthony de Mello puts it like this:

Think of someone who is afraid to let go of a nightmare
because, after all, that is the only world he knows.
There you have a picture of yourself and other people.[59]

Yet, at some deeper level, we know that we can't control the future,
that we must relinquish our tight hold on life. On a solitary retreat,
during which we're separated, to some extent, from the hooks on
which we habitually hang our anxieties and preoccupations, we
can begin to investigate and face up to our fears. We can begin
to let go of control. I've found that nature offers us clues in this
respect. For example, on a meditation retreat, I was standing on a
little bridge with a friend, watching the river flowing towards the
distant hills, as the sun was setting. 'That's the past', my friend
said, pointing forwards in the direction we were facing, towards
the hills and the sun. And he jerked his thumb over his shoulder
without looking back. 'And that's the future.' His comment rather
shocked me at the time! Normally we suppose that we look ahead
into our future. We can imagine it mapped out in front of us. But
no. Our future is rushing up behind us, and we can't see it until
it is passing under our feet.

Our grumbling, semi-conscious anxiety has often little to do
with the details it latches upon. Such anxiety often points to more
profound fears. Our death, for example, 'that undiscovered country
from whose bourne no traveller returns',[60] in Hamlet's words, can
be such a terrifying prospect because the time of its coming, its
nature, and its aftermath are so unknown. As Buddhists, we can
'plan' for our deaths by living as meritorious lives as possible,
but we can't plan for our deaths in the way we can plan for our
holidays. We *just don't know* if the afterlife takes traveller's cheques.
We *really don't know* whether to pack the sunblock or the woolly
hat. And this unknowing, this inability to control the time or nature
or, particularly, the aftermath of our deaths, is truly frightening.
But rather than allowing fear of death to grumble away on an

unconscious or semi-conscious level, rather than running to habitual, anxious preoccupations, the Buddhist is asked to face up to this fear, to acknowledge death and the brevity of life, and to allow this acknowledgement to foster a sense of urgency. Traditionally, in Buddhism, it is often isolated and wild places that are recommended to most effectively face our deepest fears. Since the Buddha's time, for example, Buddhists have meditated alone in graveyards and cremation grounds. These graveyards tend not to be the relatively tidy and ordered affairs with which we're familiar in the West, but dreadful places full of charred cloth, bones, and bodies in various stages of decomposition. In addition, there would be various spirits hanging around, so these would be truly terrifying places to sit and meditate. Until deforestation threatened their traditional way of life, the wandering forest monks of Thailand were inspiring examples of Buddhist practitioners who sought out such places in order to face up to fear.

In *Forest Recollections*, Kamala Tiyavanich gives a fascinating account of the lives of these forest monks. In one passage, he tells the story of Cha, who, meditating alone in a cremation ground, heard strange footsteps behind him and realized that he was being visited by a malignant spirit. In that moment, we're told, Cha experienced the greatest fear of his life. At first, in his panic, his spiritual practice was forgotten, but then he managed to regain his mindfulness and began to reflect:

> 'What am I so afraid of anyway?' a voice inside me asked.
>
> 'I'm afraid of death,' another voice answered.
>
> 'Well then, where is this thing "death"? Why all the panic? Look where death abides. Where is death?'
>
> 'Why death is within me!'

'If death is within you, then where are you going to run
to escape it? If you run away you die, if you stay here
you die. Wherever you go it goes with you because
death lies within you, there's nowhere you can run to.
Whether you are afraid or not you die just the same,
there's nowhere to escape death.'[61]

Another fear for the wandering forest monks was the possibility
of being attacked by wild animals – particularly wild elephants
and tigers. The roar of a nearby tiger was perhaps one of the
most frightening sounds to be heard on their wanderings, but
the monks trained themselves to hear the noise without reacting
to it. It was just another sound, coming from the forest, and then
receding back into it. To face fear more directly, some monks put
themselves in decidedly risky situations, including the indomitable
Cha, who ignored the advice of villagers and deliberately spent
the night beside an unprotected forest trail. Sure enough, in the
middle of the night, a tiger visited the monk and came so close
that Cha could actually hear it breathing. Again, Cha overcame his
fear by reflecting on death, by considering that he would have to
die anyway, and it was more meaningful to die for the Dharma.
Eventually the tiger sloped off. If Cha had panicked, he would
surely have lost his life. The experience of those monks who
survived the wilderness in this way (admittedly we don't hear a
lot about those who didn't) confirmed their faith in the Dharma.
Forest Recollections cites many examples of fierce animals who
were strangely pacified by the mindfulness and loving-kindness
of the monks. Finding themselves, whether deliberately or not, in
terrifying situations, many of the forest monks learnt to calm their
minds through reflection or intense concentration, gain wisdom,
and learn to face their fear with mindfulness. Some of these monks
developed such courage and tranquillity of mind that

they were fit to live anywhere, go anywhere, and rest anywhere, no longer troubled by fear.[62]

How much should we seek out fear on a solitary retreat? Should we be placing ourselves in the path of tigers and malignant graveyard ghosts, or our own twenty-first-century urban equivalents? This really depends on our states of mind. Reflection on death, for example, has always been a traditional Buddhist practice, and it's a practice, as I've intimated, that we might find effective and useful. But it's also a practice that is dependent on being in calm and positive states of mind. As we've seen, generating such states comprises the initial stage of a solitary retreat – or indeed a spiritual life. Even so, such positive states of mind don't necessarily mean we won't experience fear. If we're practising at all effectively, and pushing at the boundaries of entrenched habit and fixed self-view, fear will inevitably arise. But it will be a more conscious and manageable fear than the grumbling, underground anxiety that tends to assail us much of the time. It will be a fear that, hopefully, we have the positivity to sit with and not run from. Courage is not about not experiencing fear. It's about not running from it. My teacher Sangharakshita, the Buddha, and Milarepa all experienced fear when they were practising intensely. In one of his songs, Milarepa sings of trembling with fear when he hears the roar of a tigress. But, as Sangharakshita says, commenting on this episode,

> It is important to remember that being fearless does not mean that you never feel fear. The point is that even while [Milarepa] doesn't suppress his natural human reactions, he is able to be happy in the experience of fear. It is as though he relishes the roar of the tigress. His fearlessness does not exclude the experience of fear; he actually enjoys the fear that, as an embodied being, he naturally feels.[63]

Enjoy our fear? There is something about fear that is very akin to excitement. In fact, next time we're afraid, it might be worthwhile to label the feeling 'excitement' rather than 'fear' and see if it alters our perception of it. In letting go of habit and control, in pushing at the boundaries of fixed self-view, new possibilities open up. Our experience is suddenly more spacious, less limiting. Frightening, yes, but also exciting.

Yet it must be said that intense fear, when it arises, can feel debilitating, even, at times, overwhelming. Those of us who've experienced panic attacks can readily testify to this. What do we do when such terror arises? Intense fear can be triggered by a multitude of things – a thought, a memory, an association, a sound . . . What makes it more difficult to deal with is that we usually add all sorts of fearful thoughts to this *initial* flash of fear. We fear the fear and this sets up a cycle that can seem difficult to break, partly because the process happens so quickly, and we are so unaware of it. The key to dealing with this kind of fear is mindfulness. On solitary retreats, for example, when there's the possibility that our minds are less cluttered, we have the chance to more clearly see the process in action, observe what triggers the initial fear, and notice how we so readily add fearful thoughts to that initial experience. Such mindfulness often just breaks the panicky cycle.

Yet, often, fear can arise from the depths of our being without having an obvious source. It feels deep-rooted and irrational. I remember on one solitary retreat being terrified that I wouldn't get home before darkness fell. It was a terror that seemed deep and primordial. In cases like this, it is most effective just to experience the fear without running from it or investigating it. We just let it come and go. This can be a very valuable practice, though quite difficult. Our tendency is to demand that the fear have a source or a hook – so that we can see it, solve it, control it. On solitary retreats, away from many of the habitual hooks upon which we hang our fear, we may just have to sit with it.

This was what the Buddha advised in his *Discourse on Fear and Dread*. In this text, he recalls his own experience when, in the course of deliberately seeking out terrifying places to practise, he had to cope with terror:

> when fear and terror came while I was walking back
> and forth, I would not stand or sit or lie down. I would
> keep walking back and forth until I had subdued that
> fear and terror. When fear and terror came while I was
> standing, I would not walk or sit or lie down. I would
> keep standing until I had subdued that fear and terror.
> When fear and terror came while I was sitting, I would
> not lie down or stand up or walk. I would keep sitting
> until I had subdued that fear and terror. When fear and
> terror came while I was lying down, I would not sit up
> or stand or walk. I would keep lying down until I had
> subdued that fear and terror.[64]

In other words, he'd carry on with whatever he was doing. When the Buddha uses the word 'subdued' here, he doesn't mean repress. He would neither push the fear away nor investigate it, just let it come and go. Normally, when we experience a flash of intense fear, the tendency is to stop what we're doing, sit down, have a brandy, try and understand what the hell happened. Here the Buddha is saying that often the best way to deal with fear is just to experience it, carry on with what we're doing, and trust that it will pass.

The *Discourse on Fear and Dread* is also interesting in that the Buddha says that fear is conditioned by unethical action. If we experience fear in 'isolated forest or wilderness dwellings', it's because our minds are agitated by hatred, neurotic desire, jealousy, and so on. When we think of the real villains of history or literature, the Stalins and the Macbeths, what strikes us is their paranoia, their terror. They would make lousy hermits, solitaries, or contemplatives. In the *Discourse on Fear and Dread*, one of the things the Buddha is saying is that, if we are experiencing intense fear, we should examine our ethical lives.

Learning the ropes

Being on solitary retreat could be seen as a skill like any other, a practice that we can develop. So it's useful to take advice from those who have spent time on 'solitaries' and who have learnt to practise effectively. 'Don't do too much' is one piece of advice I was given, advice that came too late for one of my first solitary retreats in which I tried to pack in an enormous amount of activities: Dharma study, lots of meditation, listening to music, reading, writing, cooking, going for walks, and so on. I used those seven days to squeeze in all the things there didn't seem enough time for at home. Not surprisingly, I had a difficult retreat and came away with a blazing head. Usually it goes against the grain not to do things. Even on a solitary retreat we may find ourselves curiously busy, even if that busy-ness is concerned with 'spiritual activities'. Solitary adepts, including Milarepa, have been well aware of the tendency, and emphasize the need to declutter, to let go of our habitual, often frantic activity, even if that activity seems to be serving the Dharma.

As well as taking advice from others, we can also read books by, and about, those who have spent time in seclusion, and whose words and example can inspire, guide, or point out possible pitfalls. One book that – perhaps surprisingly – gave me an insight into how to practise more effectively on solitary retreats was *A Voyage for Madmen*, Peter Nichols' account of the 1968 Golden Globe single-handed yacht race round the world. I'd known about this race for many years, the leader on my ordination course having given a memorable talk about one of the competitors, Donald Crowhurst. Crowhurst had entered the race, hoping to win the cash prize and boost his failing business. But his boat was woefully unprepared and he secretly abandoned the race while radioing false positions to the organizers. In this way he hoped to appear to circumnavigate the globe – while actually never leaving the Atlantic. At first, it seemed that Crowhurst was making amazing progress and breaking records. It looked as if the rank outsider was going to win the race. But then the reports stopped coming in. A search began. And, eventually, Crowhurst's yacht was found – abandoned in the middle of the Atlantic. Two logbooks were discovered on board, one detailing his false positions, the other giving Crowhurst's true positions – and his true feelings. The second log ends in insane ramblings, terrible declarations of anguish. Those vast expanses of sea and sky must have heightened the unbearable tension of his deception, and it seems clear that Crowhurst threw himself overboard.

> Now is revealed the true
> nature and purpose and power
> of the game my offence I am
> I am what I am and I
> see the nature of my offence.[65]

Crowhurst's story was salutary and dramatic, but the stories of the other competitors were just as intriguing. Among others, there was Chay Blyth who, on departure day, hardly knew how to sail. For Blyth and John Ridgway, another competitor, the voyage was simply one of endurance. There was Nigel Tetley, whose boat began to break up tantalizingly close to home. The perceived failure threw a tragic shadow over the rest of his life. There was the hardy and resourceful Robin Knox-Johnson, who was the only one to finish and who donated his winnings to Crowhurst's family. And there was also the Frenchman Bernard Moitessier, who enjoyed himself so much that he abandoned the race – and just kept sailing.

A Voyage for Madmen begins with a quotation from Joseph Conrad: 'Everything can be found at sea, according to the spirit of your quest.'[66] It's interesting that Knox-Johnson and Moitessier, the two men who loved the sea, who read about it, who were inspired by it and fascinated by its shifting moods, were the ones who were truly successful – even if the Frenchman didn't officially finish the race. A mere spirit of determined endurance, a passionate desire to win the race, a desire for reputation or money – these things weren't enough to see the other competitors through and, in some cases, actually destroyed them. Reflecting on the book just before I went on a solitary retreat, I realized that solitude has really to be enjoyed for its own sake. If we go into the wilds on a solitary retreat too much in a spirit of endurance, wilfulness or goal-orientation (fame and money being less of a draw perhaps), then difficulties will arise. Yes, we want to engage with our minds and generate positive emotion. We want to change ourselves. But there is something in us that responds to solitude in nature for its own sake, and not for what we can squeeze out of it. This is Bernard Moitessier (the 'Joshua' he refers to is his boat):

> I felt such a need to rediscover the wind of the
> high sea, nothing else counted at the moment . . .
> All 'Joshua' and I wanted was to be left alone with
> ourselves. You do not ask a tame seagull why it needs
> to disappear from time to time towards the open sea.
> It goes, that's all.[67]

Another connection I made between *A Voyage for Madmen* and solitary retreats concerned the subject of ethics: how solitude often gives us a heightened awareness of our ethical lives (as we've seen, this is a point the Buddha addressed in his *Discourse on Fear and Dread*). Donald Crowhurst had nowhere, and nobody, to escape to. Sea and sky constantly led him back to his own mind, and to his own duplicity. Moitessier, on the other hand, who set to sea with a certain purity of motive, relished the solitude and the vast spaces, and often experienced blissful states of mind. It seems to me important to go on a solitary retreat, especially when we're not very used to periods alone in nature, in good states of mind, and with a positive motivation (to the extent we're aware of our motivation). In this way we can more readily enjoy solitude for its own sake. Conversely, I'm not sure that solitary retreats are necessarily the best places to dig ourselves out of particularly negative or unskilful states of mind, especially our first solitaries. If we try to do that, we may come to associate solitude primarily with painful states of mind.

Another book I've drawn upon for inspiration as regards solitary retreats is Vicki Mackenzie's *Cave in the Snow*, an account of the life of the Englishwoman Diane Perry, who became known by her Tibetan name, Tenzin Palmo, and who spent twelve years in solitary seclusion in a Himalayan cave. During her time in the cave, she had to deal with intense cold, wild animals, near starvation, and avalanches. At one point she became entombed by a snowfall, but eventually managed to dig herself to safety using a saucepan lid. Yet, despite the ascetic life and the duration of her retreat, she was never lonely. In fact, she declares in the book that she was far lonelier in the Tibetan monastery where she was the lone nun among a hundred monks, and had to struggle against traditional prejudices against women.

The book is inspiring on many levels. Reading *Cave in the Snow* strengthened my confidence that spending time in solitude is well worth the effort – indeed, that spiritual life in general is well worth the effort. The book is also a very good antidote to certain doubts that may arise in our minds now and then, one of them being 'is solitude an escape from real life?' As we'll see later, solitude can indeed be an escape from responsibility and from the sometimes painful business of forging connections with others, but to the question of whether going to a cave isn't 'an evasion of the trials of "ordinary life"', Tenzin Palmo replies:

> Not at all. To my mind worldly life is an escape . . . When you have a problem you can turn on the television, phone a friend, go out for a coffee. In a cave, however, you have no one to turn to but yourself. When problems arise and things get tough you have no choice but to go through with them, and come out the other side. In a cave you face your own nature in the raw, you have to find a way of working with it and dealing with it.[68]

Another doubt we may have regarding solitude is whether it's a selfish activity. After all, here we are sitting 'looking at our navels', not appearing to help anybody . . . But whether time spent in solitude is an egocentric activity or not depends on our motivation. With Tenzin Palmo, we don't have the sense of a selfish woman at all. In fact, reading *Cave in the Snow*, we have a sense that her whole practice is founded upon developing compassion for others. At one point she talks about her meetings with the 'Togdens', the wild-looking, dreadlocked, and extremely friendly Buddhist yogis who were selected for particularly rigorous training. These highly impressive practitioners told Tenzin Palmo that, for the first three years of their training, they were told simply to watch their minds and to develop Bodhicitta, that is, a compassion for all beings and a desire for their Enlightenment. This was the foundation of their practice. Tenzin Palmo came out of her twelve-year retreat and engaged in unceasing compassionate activity. But that compassionate activity was partly a result of twelve years spent in solitude. It is a seeming paradox of spiritual life that time spent on one's own, sometimes in seclusion, is one of the factors that enable us to develop love and compassion for others.

Yet, even if somebody like Tenzin Palmo spent their whole life in seclusion, I think they could be said to be serving a useful function. The world needs its hermits and its solitaries. They serve as an example, inspiration, and corrective to a world that is so caught up in acquisition and ceaseless, anxious activity. And who knows what effect such solitary practitioners may be having, or will continue to have, on the world outside their caves and huts. One thousand years after his death, the cotton-clad, cave-dwelling yogi Milarepa is still inspiring others with his songs of spiritual joy.

Tenzin Palmo was reluctant to talk in *Cave in the Snow* about her meditation experiences. She certainly experienced a lot of bliss and happiness during her twelve-year sojourn, but she insisted that bliss was valuable only as a launching point for developing insight into the nature of reality. It was not to be pursued as an end in itself. On solitary retreats we can become too *experience*-motivated and try to chase positive states, rather than slowly learning about our own mind, patiently seeing into the nature of our habit and fear, allowing a sense of spaciousness to develop as we let go of our tendency to identify with our thoughts and habits. We have a sense reading *Cave in the Snow* of someone who has let go of rigid habit – and of expectation. Tenzin Palmo seemed to be able to let go of expectations of how her long retreat, or her future, should proceed, accepting whatever arose, externally or internally, with equanimity. Before we set off on a solitary retreat we might find that we're hoping for all sorts of things from our time away. We may be expecting that certain positive states of mind will arise. It's important not to force any kind of outcome on our solitary retreat, but to set off with a curious heart, see what arises, and let the retreat take its own course.

As with Milarepa, Tenzin Palmo can be an inspiration for us without our feeling we have to replicate her experience. After all, she was an exceptional woman, temperamentally suited to solitude, and we don't have to literally haul ourselves up to a cave and spend twelve years there to gain encouragement from her life. But, at the very least, she can be an inspiration in training in the capacity to be alone in our own room. Or in beginning to experiment with spending time alone in nature. But how long should we spend on our own in this way? Not many people could, or should, endure twelve years in a cave, and it's debatable how useful prolonged solitary retreats are, particularly for Westerners. We're usually advised to start with short periods of solitude, a weekend if we're really unused to being alone in nature, then perhaps a week, a fortnight . . . If we find our time away has been useful and effective, we might decide to go on longer solitary retreats – a month, three months. Some Buddhist friends have gone on solitary retreats for a year or more, but longer solitaries have to be worked up to. When I was first ordained as a Buddhist, I tended to be a little wilful and goal-orientated, and I decided to go on a three-month solitary. Although I learnt a lot about myself, I ended up feeling quite isolated by the end, and was forced to swallow my pride and come home a fortnight early. It was too much too soon. Partly the duration of a retreat will depend on our temperament. Some of us are more suited to solitude than others. And partly we will learn, through trial and error, what is an appropriate duration for us.

There is also the question of whether we should have a routine or not on solitary retreat. Again, this may partly depend on temperament, but it might be advisable, on our first solitary retreats, to adhere to a timetable of walks, meditation, ritual, or whatever (without, of course, feeling a slave to that routine). But routine may not suit everybody. I have one friend who is very practised at solitary retreats. He works as a builder, on and off, for part of the year and, for the rest of the year, goes on solitary. My friend is very adaptable on these retreats. A particular day will require a particular meditation practice. He will vary his walks every day because he finds that, if he repeats a walk too often, his mind becomes a little dull. He is very aware of his energy levels and what particular practice he might need to effectively engage with them. He's very aware too of what food does to his body and mind, and what should be on the menu on a particular day. And he tends to know, quite intuitively, on which days he should put in a lot of effort, and on which days he should rest . . . For myself, less well versed in solitary retreats, I prefer to do the same things at the same time each day. I like the simplicity of that, the freedom from the kind of choice that can tyrannize us, particularly in the city.

Another question, very pertinent to this book, a question I've asked quite a few of my friends who regularly do solitary retreats, is: how do we deal with loneliness on solitary? We've answered this, to some extent, in the previous chapter. As we've seen, the tendency is to run from loneliness to distraction and habit. On solitary retreat, with far fewer distractions present than at home, we are more obliged to just sit with that tension, to let loneliness season us to some extent. On solitary retreat too, away from those closest to us, we may have no choice but to learn to enjoy being with ourselves, to develop more loving-kindness towards ourselves. But a common experience on solitary retreat, a common realization, is that we're feeling lonely because we haven't made enough of our connections and friendships with those back home. Being on a solitary retreat does make us examine our heart connections, and it's the rare person who can say that they feel they have loved family and friends to the very best of their ability. So one of the ways of dealing with loneliness on a solitary retreat is to resolve, on our return, to connect more with those we love; to be less superficial, more open, and more generous.

We've seen that our loneliness and isolation are dependent on having an ego. So it's not surprising that so many of us have discovered that empathy and love, a reaching out beyond self-concern, are the way out of loneliness on solitary retreat. There seems to come a point for many of us on solitary when we realize that, for our retreat to have any true meaning, we must practise for the benefit of others, as well as for ourselves. Usually we have known this theoretically, but at some point we *feel* it. As Buddhists we are practising in a context: with others and for others. The way out of loneliness or isolation, then, is to love more deeply. And the rest of the book is really concerned with this.

Lost in the wilds

The Buddha's main attendant was called Ananda, and he served the Buddha with great devotion and loyalty for many years. But before Ananda, there were other attendants, not all of whom were quite up to the job. In the Meghiya Sutta, we hear of one such man, Meghiya, who, coming across a delightful mango grove on his alms round, decided that this would be the ideal place to exert himself alone in meditation. So he asked the Buddha's permission to be relieved of his duties so that he could go there and practise. The Buddha asked Meghiya to wait until somebody else could replace him, but Meghiya was insistent, reminding the Buddha that he was Enlightened, while he (Meghiya) was not and still had much work to do. Finally the Buddha told Meghiya to 'Do what you think it is now time to do',[69] so Meghiya went off to the mango grove and, basically, had a very difficult time. He just couldn't concentrate. He was plagued by distraction, desire, and ill will. Meghiya then went back to the Buddha with his tail between his legs, and asked his teacher what went wrong.

The *Meghiya Sutta* touches on a lot of very interesting themes, and I don't have the space here to investigate the Buddha's response to Meghiya's aborted solitary retreat in any great detail. But it seems that it wasn't really time for Meghiya to go off on solitary, that his heart was immature. And one of the ways the Buddha suggested that Meghiya, and we, 'mature the heart', was through a commitment to spiritual friendship. Through spiritual friendship, through communion with those who are committed to the same path as ourselves, we are able to have ourselves reflected back to ourselves. Through the inspiration and example of spiritual friends, and through communication with them, we are more easily able to develop. In particular, our ethical sensibility can more easily flourish. Meghiya failed in his responsibilities to his spiritual friend, the Buddha. Nor did he seem to realize the unique chance he possessed for spiritual growth through being around his Enlightened teacher. He evidently didn't know himself very well and didn't understand why one practises in a context with others. He didn't understand that to really come to know oneself, one needs other people. For us the lesson of this text might be, not that we shouldn't do solitary retreats when we're first starting on the Buddhist path, but that such retreats should take place in a context, particularly in a context of spiritual friendship. A spiritual friend may be able to point out our blind spots. They may be able to give us much useful advice as to when, for example, the time might be right for embarking on a solitary retreat.

We know that Meghiya came from a noble family but we don't know much else about him. We don't know his age, for example, but I imagine him as quite a young man. I also see him as very idealistic, and rather arrogant. Perhaps he was similar in temperament to Chris McCandless, the young American from a well-to-do family who was drawn to testing himself, in solitude, in wild and inaccessible places. In April 1992, at the age of twenty-four, McCandless set off on his biggest adventure.

He hitched to Alaska and walked alone into the wilderness. He'd abandoned almost all of his possessions and, in creating a new life for himself, he'd also given himself a new name – Alexander Supertramp. Fiercely independent, strong-willed, and capable of extreme physical endurance, McCandless was determined, as one of the last people to see him alive recalled, 'to prove to himself that he could make it on his own, without anybody's help'.[70]

> AND NOW AFTER TWO RAMBLING YEARS
> COMES THE FINAL AND GREATEST ADVENTURE.
> THE CLIMACTIC BATTLE TO KILL THE FALSE
> BEING WITHIN AND VICTORIOUSLY CONCLUDE
> THE SPIRITUAL REVOLUTION. TEN DAYS AND
> NIGHTS OF FREIGHT TRAINS AND HITCH-
> HIKING BRING HIM TO THE GREAT WHITE
> NORTH. NO LONGER TO BE POISONED BY
> CIVILIZATION HE FLEES, AND WALKS ALONE
> UPON THE LAND TO BECOME LOST IN THE WILD
> – ALEXANDER SUPERTRAMP. MAY 1992.[71]

This was McCandless's declaration of independence, scrawled on a piece of plywood in the deserted old bus that became his shelter. He had stumbled across the bus in a clearing near the Sushana River and, using it as his base, he lived off the land, picking berries, plants, and roots, and, although he was ambivalent about killing animals, hunting game. In his youthful idealism, he was perhaps convinced of his own invincibility, but he made some serious mistakes. He had no compass and was generally very ill-prepared for his time in the wilderness. He had set out without adequate food, clothes, or tools. In his desire to inhabit uncharted territory he had even abandoned his map. After three months, he decided to leave, but his trail was blocked by the Teklanika River, which was now higher and swifter than when he'd crossed it. Without a map McCandless was trapped, and eventually he starved to death. His body was found in the bus a month later.

The story of Chris McCandless is told by Jon Krakauer in his book, *Into the Wild* (the book was also made into a film directed by Sean Penn). The book is far more than the dramatic, and ultimately tragic, story of a young man who overreached himself. It is an eloquent meditation on solitude, wilderness, loneliness, and the desire to go beyond one's limits – and access some kind of spiritual state in the process. Krakauer, a mountaineer, and drawn to adventure, danger, and wilderness himself, tells the tale without judgement and, as readers, we too suspend our judgement. Though we have a sense from the book that McCandless could be arrogant, cold-hearted, and very judgemental himself, it's impossible not to admire his courage, resourcefulness, and idealism. At the end of the book, we have a sense of tragic waste. And perhaps it's a particularly American tragedy, conditioned, as it is, by a view that is especially strong in North America (and in most New World or pioneering societies). McCandless made a great mistake in ditching his map, but that mistake came from a view, the view that individuals can be entirely self-sufficient and autonomous. We hear echoes of that view in the words of some of the writers who've accompanied us on our journey – Thoreau, Emerson, and Emily Dickinson. Though, as I hope we've seen, we can gain much from reading these writers, ultimately the idea of an entirely autonomous and independent soul does not sit easily with Buddhism.

If McCandless had lived, he would undoubtedly have mellowed. In fact, we already find evidence of this in the books and notebooks that were discovered in the bus where he died. In his copy of the Russian novel *Doctor Zhivago*, Boris Pasternak states:

> You can't make such discoveries without spiritual
> equipment. And the basic elements of this equipment
> are the Gospels. What are they? To begin with, <u>love of
> one's neighbour</u>.[72]

The underlining is McCandless's. Another passage in the novel
reads:

> And so it turned out that only a life similar to the life
> of those around us, merging with it without a ripple,
> is genuine life, and that an unshared happiness is not
> happiness . . . And this was most vexing of all.[73]

Next to this passage McCandless wrote: 'HAPPINESS ONLY
REAL WHEN SHARED'.[74] A Buddhist would say that it's possible,
and desirable, to be happy on our own on a solitary retreat. But
it's impossible not to desire that happiness for others too. Chris
McCandless, at the very end of his life, had wanted to share what
he had learnt from his adventures. He had begun to realize that,
although we are essentially alone, we are also essentially related.

5

Relatedness

Alone with Others

I am in you and you in me, mutual in love divine.[75]

William Blake

'It is as if a hand has come out and taken yours'

The Miracle Worker is a film (originally a stage play) that dramatizes the early life of Helen Keller, an American author, political activist, and lecturer. When she was nineteen months old, Keller developed a severe illness that resulted in her becoming deaf and blind. In the film we observe Helen, as an older girl, locked into her dark and silent world, unable to communicate, frustrated and isolated. Her loving family eventually employ a teacher, Anne Sullivan, herself partially sighted, who attempts to communicate with Helen through spelling out words into her hand. The teacher's attempts are frustrated by Helen's family, who tend to spoil and pamper the girl, but Anne Sullivan persuades them to let her take Helen away with her to a summer house for an extended stay, hoping that this will provide the conditions necessary for a breakthrough. Helen is furious to be torn away from her family, and exhibits her characteristic fiery temper and iron will, refusing to cooperate with her teacher. Through an unsentimental firmness of purpose, however, Anne Sullivan manages to teach Helen a certain amount of obedience, as well as get her to repeat and spell out some of the hand signs for objects. But the hand signs are all just a game to Helen, a game of right and wrong, reward and punishment. She doesn't realize that Anne Sullivan is attempting to convey the gift of language itself. Eventually, Helen is handed back to her family with no real breakthrough having taken place, and Anne Sullivan begins to see any gains that have been made slowly being eroded, as Helen reasserts her will over her more pliant family. Towards the end of the film, in despair and frustration, Sullivan grabs Helen and holds her under the water pump in the garden, deluging her with water and then signing W-A-T-E-R on her hand. She does this again and again, as Helen struggles in rage and fear. The moment that follows is probably one of the most moving I've ever seen on film. Helen suddenly stops fighting under the pump. She goes silent for a few seconds, as understanding begins to dawn. She furiously begins to pump the water herself and then spells W-A-T-E-R into Sullivan's hand. Then, wildly, she begins to touch object after object, demanding to know the name and hand sign for each. And Sullivan signs for her – P-U-M-P, T-R-E-E, S-T-E-P, B-E-L-L . . . and, finally, M-A-M-A and P-A-P-A. As her parents embrace Helen, Anne Sullivan lets out a cry of triumph: 'She knows!' The hand signs are no longer a game. In truly understanding one word, Helen has understood language itself. She has broken out of her isolation. Suddenly, empathy is possible, true love is possible – and gratitude is possible. Helen breaks from her parents' embrace, turns to Anne Sullivan, and touches her with her finger. Who, she wants to know, is she? Anne Sullivan spells it out into Helen's hand and then Helen reciprocates: T-E-A-C-H-E-R.

To me, the life of Helen Keller, as dramatically depicted in *The Miracle Worker*, is a powerful metaphor for the Buddhist life. This seeming fixed and rigid self of ours, according to Buddhism, is an illusion, but it is an illusion that has such a fierce hold on us that we are deaf and blind to our true nature, our vast potential. The Buddha's teaching is exclusively concerned with helping beings emerge from this darkness, break out of the isolating and imprisoning shell of the ego. One of the most significant moments in Buddhist history came when the Buddha managed to communicate his insight to one of his disciples, Kondanna. Until that moment, the Buddha was uncertain if his Enlightenment experience could be passed on at all, so, when the light dawned on his disciple, the Buddha gave a great cry of triumph, a lion's roar: 'Kondanna knows!'

We are not told of Kondanna's response to his teacher after his Awakening, but it would certainly have been one of overwhelming gratitude. Gratitude, which is the precursor to worship, is a connecting emotion, a positive quality that begins to move us away from isolation. The more we acknowledge the worth of our teachers and of their teachings, the less lonely we become. And the more we acknowledge the worth of what has been given to us, the more we will want to pass it on, just as the Buddha's disciples passed on his teachings, and just as Helen Keller passed on what Anne Sullivan had communicated to her. As Sangharakshita says in *The Yogi's Joy*:

> Gratitude opens us up to the fact of our
> interconnectedness with others. Whenever we enjoy
> or achieve something, it is salutary to recognize
> and acknowledge the work and kindness of all the
> individuals who have contributed to it. But gratitude
> to the guru has an extra dimension, because what we
> are grateful for is beyond valuation. There is no hope
> of repaying the debt, except by passing the gift on to
> others.[76]

We have seen that we are essentially alone. The Buddha exhorted his disciples to be lamps unto themselves. We are born alone, we die alone, and we are responsible for our own actions, and for our own spiritual development. But, as well as being essentially alone, we're also essentially related. Helen Keller could not have broken out of her isolation without Anne Sullivan's patience and determination. The Buddhist life is impossible without teachers, guidance, and support. When we look at a painting of Milarepa, or read one of his supremely confident and joyful songs, we feel that we're looking at, and listening to, somebody who is utterly self-sufficient. In a way this is true, but every one of Milarepa's songs is prefaced by loving, devotional verses directed towards his teacher, Marpa, the man who freed Milarepa from darkness and isolation. In a sense, Marpa *created* Milarepa and Milarepa is, quite literally, eternally grateful.

In our more deluded moments, we tend to regard ourselves as pretty self-sufficient individuals with our own unique thoughts and our own finely honed system of beliefs. But this tendency is indeed a delusion. In writing this book, for example, I've become very aware to what extent thoughts and ideas, which I'd assumed were my own, were, in fact, my teacher's. Time and again, I've put down some observation with which I've been rather pleased, only to uncover the very same observation later in one of Sangharakshita's books or seminars. Perhaps I absorbed many of these thoughts semi-consciously many years ago. It can feel slightly humiliating, but I think it's a positive thing. It shows I've been receptive to my teacher's influence. The wise light the way for us, help us to break through barriers of isolation, ignorance, and loneliness, by articulating what has hitherto been inarticulate, or only half-formed, in our minds. In the very act of communication, good teachers can demonstrate that we are related, that it's possible for human beings to understand one another. Much of the time, self-concern gets in the way of true communication but, if we are receptive enough, we will feel the hand of wisdom touch our own. A good teacher – and sometimes the most unlikely person may assume that role for us – will demonstrate that, although we are alone, this aloneness is not particular to us. We are essentially in the same boat. We all must experience joy and pain, be separated from those we love, and, eventually, we must die. A good teacher will show that we are related in this very essential way, by virtue of our common humanity. And, in understanding this, we will feel less isolated.

The playwright Alan Bennett (who writes so well on the subject of loneliness) wrote a very well-acclaimed and popular play called *The History Boys*. The play examines the following question: what constitutes authentic and what, inauthentic, education? Perhaps the play captured the popular imagination because Hector, the main character, exemplified, for many, the kind of inspirational teacher they'd yearned for, and, in some cases, been lucky enough to have. Hector's recurring exhortation to his pupils is to 'pass it on':

> Pass the parcel. That's sometimes all you can do. Take it, feel it and pass it on. Not for me, not for you but for someone, somewhere, one day.[77]

In one scene, Hector is giving an extracurricular poetry lesson to one of his pupils, Posner. The scene is made more poignant by the fact that both Hector and Posner are quite lonely individuals who almost, but don't quite, manage to connect (in the production of the play that I saw their hands literally reach out – but don't quite touch). In the course of the lesson, Hector passes on this insight to Posner:

> The best moments in reading are when you come
> across something – a thought, a feeling, a way of
> looking at things – which you had thought special and
> particular to you. Now here it is, set down by someone
> else, a person you have never met, someone even who
> is long dead. And it is as if a hand has come out and
> taken yours.[78]

The great poets, sages, and spiritual teachers offer us their hands. These hands might not necessarily be comforting – Marpa's hand was rough and coarse, and Anne Sullivan needed to resort to a very firm hand at times – but we need to accept such hands when they're offered. Any kind of human development and progress is impossible without the supporting hands of teachers. We take the inherited knowledge and wisdom of the past for granted, but even the seeming simplest of tasks, like the baking of a loaf, relies on the accumulated and hard-won knowledge of our ancestors. In the novel *Robinson Crusoe*, Crusoe reflects on

> the strange multitude of little things necessary in the
> providing, producing, curing, dressing, making, and
> finishing this one article of bread.[79]

The effort Crusoe puts into the plowing, sowing, harrowing, mowing, reaping, and curing, and all the other activities necessary to make bread, is truly heroic but, despite this admirable self-sufficiency, he still relies on the wisdom of the past – in understanding the process by which bread is made in the first place. Chris McCandless's primary error was to believe that a human being could be entirely self-sufficient, but the fact that he drew inspiration from wise men such as Boris Pasternak or Thoreau showed that, in actuality, he had a need to have imaginative communion with minds other than his own. Indeed, some of the authors he was reading had begun to pull him back to a sense of relatedness ('HAPPINESS ONLY REAL WHEN SHARED'). But, for McCandless, it was too late. In rejecting the map that could have shown him a route out of the wilderness, he turned his back on the wisdom of the past, rejected the hand that could have guided him to safety.

It's impossible to speak of solitude without also speaking of relatedness. Paradoxically, it's often on solitary retreat that I realize how related I really am. I am always in relationship, even if 'only' imaginatively. On a solitary retreat it's often very useful to reflect on how much we owe to others, how much we owe, for example, to all those who have taught us something of value or beauty. Our selves, apparently so fixed and encrusted with personality and habit, are subtly changed by every word of affirmation or cruelty; so the more we can remain open to the influence of the wise, and the more we can resist the tendency to become hardened by habit, arrogance, and cynicism, the more our isolation will be attenuated.

In Buddhism, spiritual friendship, the attempt to empathize with another on the basis of a shared ideal, occupies a central position. The receiving and passing on of wisdom is one aspect of spiritual friendship, and is a perennial manifestation of our essential relatedness.

Alone with others

A Buddhist is committed to going beyond the ego, to addressing the fear, entrenched habit, and fixed self-view that so limits our potential. Our human tendency is to fixate on the objects of our awareness, to attach to those objects that give us pleasure, and to attempt to reject (while still fixating upon) those objects that afford us pain. In this way we become divided against ourselves

– and against others. We become blind to the fact that it is the amazing reality of awareness itself, rather than the objects of that awareness, that is the potential source of our liberation. It is this awareness that we all share and through which we are fundamentally related. The fact that, as human beings, we all share an awareness and human consciousness, might seem too obvious even to be stated. Yet we take for granted the wonderful and potentially unifying power of awareness. We concentrate instead on that which divides us. We forget the fact that we are all part of an overarching sky and we identify with very specific clouds, and argue for their overweening importance.

As Buddhists, we are attempting to stop defining ourselves so rigidly with regard to the objects of our awareness, attempting to break through the constricting and isolating shell of ego that we build up through such rigid identification. We're attempting to bring more awareness into every aspect of our lives and allow that awareness to change and transform us. This is essentially what it means to practise the Buddha's teaching, the Dharma. At different times in our lives, the Dharma can be practised in solitude, or in more direct participation with others and for the benefit of others. This book has been concerned largely with practice in solitude. In solitude, we can remove ourselves from the accretions and distractions upon which we tend to fixate, and more easily bring a transformative awareness to the fear, habit, and identifications that so limit us. In solitude we begin to face up to the fact of our essential aloneness, and to the sense of isolation and loneliness that is the product of our fixed self-view. But, if our practice in solitude is effective, as we've seen, we'll also experience a sense of our essential relatedness. We will participate imaginatively in the life of others, whether through meditation, reflection, reading, or some other means.

The other pole of practice is that of working more directly with, and for, others. As we'll see in the next section, Buddhist ethics is built around sympathy, an imaginative identification with others. For most of us, it is daily contact with other people, rather than solitude, that gives us the most frequent opportunity for practice. Altruistic activity; the bringing up of children; any loving relationship that is not based on one's own neurotic desires, but attempts to see the reality of the other; working with others on a shared project; the challenge of spiritual friendship: all these demand empathy and, if we practise effectively within such situations, they move us beyond fixed self-view and mere self-concern. And just as, in practising effectively in solitude, we realize to what extent we're related, so, when we effectively practise in relation to others, we realize to what extent we're essentially alone. In this context, Sangharakshita gives the example of spiritual friendship:

> True spiritual fellowship fosters communication in
> its most mature sense: mutual responsiveness across
> a chasm. Even though you share a heartfelt ideal,
> you are both aware that as long as there is a sense of
> separate selfhood, you will always feel an element of
> loneliness, when you are on your own and even when
> you are with a friend. Indeed, it is your shared ideal
> that reminds you of the chasm between you. The more
> that knowledge is implicit in your communication, the
> more effective the communication will be. If you are in
> a reasonably positive state of mind, such an insight will
> be exhilarating rather than depressing. A good friend is
> someone with whom you can be alone.[80]

When we truly relate to a spiritual friend, we acknowledge the separateness and autonomy of self and other. Although friends and teachers can guide us and show us the way, true spiritual friendship is based on the acknowledgement that

109

we come into the world alone and die alone, and that the friend or teacher cannot 'do' our development for us. It's only based on such an acknowledgement that true communication and connection is possible. Within the context of spiritual friendship, indeed, within the context of any mature friendship or relationship, we're working against the habitual tendency to see others in terms primarily of our own needs. When we were children our mother was an extension of our selves. We didn't see her as an autonomous individual with her own desires. We all need comfort, security, and saviours at times but, in order to develop mature relationships and friendships, we need to move on from the kind of connection of which the mother–child relationship is the most obvious example. We need to develop the kind of bracing relationship in which we are able to experience ourselves as separate, yet connected. Sam Keen, in his book *Fire in the Belly*, articulates this very well:

> True love is the only just and holy war. Two friends
> pledge loyal opposition to one another. I vow that
> I will defend the integrity of my separate being
> and respect the integrity of your being. We will
> meet only as equals; I will present myself to you in
> the fullness of my being and will expect the same
> of you. I will not cower, apologise or condescend.
> Our covenant will be to love one another justly
> and powerfully; to establish and cherish inviolable
> boundaries; to respect our separate sanctuaries. We
> will remain joined in the sweet agony of dialogue,
> the contest of conversation, the dialectic of love until
> we arrive at a synthesis.[81]

In the above passage, Keen is talking about the development of mature sexual relationships, but what he says could be just

as applicable to any mature relationship, including a spiritual
friendship. Spiritual friendship isn't always comfortable or easy; at
times, it should be challenging and, occasionally, confrontational.
As somebody who steers clear of confrontation, I tend to try and
avoid Keen's 'sweet agony of dialogue' in spiritual friendship,
but there was one particular close friend who didn't allow me to
avoid it. My friendship with him was delightful, but always edgy.
Sometimes the edginess became too much for me and I'd pull
away from him. When he moved to another city, I found I missed
him very much, and yearned again for his bracing conversation,
which had never been an expression of hatred, but one of kindness
and engagement. In its sweetness, and in its challenge, spiritual
friendship is the context through which we can perhaps feel,
most positively, alone with others. The demands and delights of
truly getting to know a fellow Dharma-farer have traditionally
been regarded, in Buddhism, as one of the most effective ways of
combating fixed self-view.

But a question arises: how much should we practise in
solitude, and how much directly with, and for, others? The
predominance of one or other aspect will partly depend on
temperament. Generally speaking, the more introverted of us
will be drawn to the more meditative, solitary, and reflective
aspects of Buddhist practice, while the more extrovert will be
drawn more to spiritual friendship, compassionate activity,
working together on the basis of shared ideals, and so on. So
where do we strike the balance? I tend to think that we should
play to our strengths and concentrate on those aspects of
practice with which we are most emotionally connected, but an
over-concentration on either aspect brings its dangers. Practice
in which altruistic activity, say, is predominant can result in
a situation where our own needs become neglected: we can
become too busy, or lose a sense of vision. To concentrate overly
on solitary activities also has its dangers. Such a concentration

can be a retreat into habit, rather than a welcoming of new possibilities. It can be a refusal, perhaps, to face the challenge of friendship or relationship. Disappearing into our room, or into nature, can feed into tendencies to self-absorption and secrecy when, at a given time, what we might really need is some basic, human companionship, or to open up to others.

Writing this short book has been very stirring in many ways. I've always presumed that I've been pretty self-sufficient and relished my own company but, in reading up for this book and attempting to clarify my thoughts, I can see that I can take my practice of solitude much further, enjoy my own company to a far greater degree. At the same time, I've also realized that I need other people much more than I care to admit. Friends, companions, even animals, bring parts of me alive that don't get nourished in solitude. So one of the things that writing this book has thrown up for me personally is the greater need to get that difficult balance right, that balance between practising – and, indeed, engaging with life – on my own, and practising – and engaging with life – in relationship with other people.

The balance between the two modes of practice will be different for all of us, but the benchmark for a Buddhist is to ask oneself if a particular practice, whether undertaken alone or with others, is *effective*. Is it working? Is it taking us beyond habit, fear, limitations, and self-concern – or is it reinforcing these things? Is it helping us develop empathy, compassion, and wisdom, or is it detracting from our development? Of course, it's not always clear to us when a particular practice is working or not, and this is when the advice of a teacher, or good friend, can be so valuable. They can point out when we are getting out of balance. The fact is that, in order to grow and develop, we need both solitary and participatory activities in our lives. As Anthony Storr says in *Solitude*:

Two opposing drives operate throughout life: the drive
for companionship, love, and everything else which
brings us close to our fellow men; and the drive toward
being independent, separate, and autonomous.[82]

That I've chosen to write about solitude, rather than the more
participatory aspects of Buddhist practice, isn't because I don't
value the latter. It's just that, arguably, solitude needs more
championing, especially at a time when silence and spaciousness
are so undervalued, when solitude is so easily assumed to be self-
centred, and when compassionate activity is necessarily equated
with socially committed projects. As I hope I've demonstrated,
solitude and altruistic activity are not mutually exclusive. When
we go deeply and effectively into one, we discover the other. For
a Buddhist, the purpose of both solitary and participatory activity
is to develop empathy and move beyond egotism.

'Join the Sangha!'

The Buddha's quest for Enlightenment was one he undertook,
to a great extent, alone. He had some teachers, it's true, but he
outstripped them fairly early on in his spiritual career. And apart
from five ascetics with whom he practised for a while, he had
no spiritual community or Sangha. My teacher, Sangharakshita,
also had to go it alone to a great extent. As the Second World War
came to an end, Sangharakshita, who was stationed with the army
in India at the time, decided to seek ordination as a Buddhist.
Buddhism, however, had all but died out in India, there was no
effective Buddhist Sangha, and, at first, Sangharakshita had only
one companion as a fellow seeker. In the end, Sangharakshita met
some important teachers whose wisdom he found invaluable, but
much of his early spiritual life was experienced in relative solitude.

It's interesting, in the light of all this, that both Sangharakshita (whose name means 'protector of the Sangha') and the Buddha emphasized the importance of Sangha and spiritual community. According to Trevor Ling, this is an emphasis that seems to have been an innovation of the Buddha himself. Ling says that, until the time of the Buddha, spiritual practice in India was more or less synonymous with solitude, and that it was only

> among the Buddhists that there soon emerged, for the
> first time in Indian history, an ordered community of
> those who were seeking for salvation from the human
> malaise as they saw it.[83]

Following the example of the Buddha, Sangharakshita emphasized, in his teaching, that the central act of a Buddhist was to commit oneself to the Three Jewels of Buddhism: to the Buddha, the Dharma, and the Sangha. This fundamental commitment is to three jewels, not two. The Sangha is not an optional extra.

Perhaps it was precisely *because* they realized how difficult it was to undertake the spiritual life on one's own that both Sangharakshita and the Buddha stressed the necessity of spiritual community, made it clear that Sangha should pervade the whole of one's spiritual life. For both the Buddha and Sangharakshita, engaging with the spiritual community is much more far-reaching than developing a supportive friendship or two. A commitment to the Sangha jewel is a commitment to a *network* of spiritual friendships based on shared values, friendships that operate on both a teacher–pupil and a peer level, and that seek to transform society for the better and, ultimately, include all beings in their embrace.

In terms of our individual development, Sangha is important for a number of reasons. We have many blind spots and it's often only a good friend, a friend who genuinely seeks our welfare, who is able, or willing, to point these faults out to us. In addition, being part of a spiritual community means that, when we let ourselves down, we also let our friends and the whole spiritual community down. In this context, the experience of shame is seen as a positive thing, and is very different from the guilt we might have grown up with as Westerners. (Indeed, it may take quite a few years before we can differentiate between such guilt and a positive sense of shame.) The desire to avoid letting down our friends and teachers gives us an added impetus to practise and behave ethically. Sangha offers us support too, a support that doesn't exclude comfort and reassurance, but that ideally offers the kind of bracing interaction we looked at in the last section, the kind of communication where we can truly be alone with others.

One could say, however, that Sangha is primarily important for a Buddhist because its creation is the reflection of *reality*. The creation of, and commitment to, Sangha is the practical application of the Buddhist belief that the fixed and permanent sense of self to which we attach is a fiction. As we've seen many times in this book, it's this sense of fixed and permanent selfhood that leads to our isolation and loneliness. But, in going beyond this isolating fiction, Buddhists are not trying to annihilate all traces of their character or individuality. Buddhism recognizes that we have a relative and provisional individuality, but it is an individuality that is dynamic, in constant flux, and that changes as conditions change. In other words, we have a pragmatic, operational self, but Buddhism differs from most other analyses of human nature in denying the absolute, permanent, or fixed nature of that self.

The spiritual community, then, encourages its members to go beyond this fixed sense of self and experience themselves in a very different, and dynamic, way. One is not being asked to *merge* with others and lose one's sense of essential aloneness. But, by forging a sense of connectedness based on shared values, and empathy for one another, members of the Sangha are being encouraged to realize that, as well as being fundamentally alone, we human beings are also fundamentally related. This realization is radical and transformative. As Trevor Ling puts it:

> The Sangha, therefore, provides the environment in which a new dimension of consciousness becomes possible as a result of the denial, not only in theory but also in practice, of the idea of *absolute* and *permanent* individuality.[84]

Practically speaking, in order to address fixed self-view and bring about this 'new dimension of consciousness', sharing and generosity must play fundamental parts in the Buddhist life. The word 'bhikkhu', which was used to refer to the Buddha's followers, literally means 'shares man'. The robes, food, shelter, and necessities that were provided by the lay people did not *belong* to the monks and nuns. Everything was shared. And in our modern, complex society the Buddhist life, as we've seen in previous chapters, still demands renunciation and sharing. As Buddhists we are asked to give, and to relinquish our tight hold on possessions. In monasteries, fellowships, and communities, Buddhists have been, and remain, faced with the difficult task of subjugating their egos in order to further the harmony and unity of the spiritual community, and promote a common vision. This vision is not based upon mere conformity, but upon a shared ethical foundation, upon sharing and generosity – and upon empathy.

Fixed self-view cuts deep. Others are too often seen as satellites revolving around *our* sun, sometimes attractive, sometimes repulsive, but rarely seen as stars in their own right. Our self-concern blinds us to the realization that we're made up of the same stardust. To counteract such self-concern, Buddhist practice encourages an imaginative identification with others. As

Stephen Batchelor says in his excellent book *Alone with Others*, it's only through such continual empathy that self-centredness is transcended and we come to realize how related we really are:

> Through the sustained contemplation of the equality
> of self and other we descend to a depth at which we
> suddenly touch that essential reality: we are with
> others. This primal experience reveals that the presence
> of others is not incidental but essential to our being.
> We do not just happen to 'bump into' others but are
> inescapably together with them in the world. As this
> awareness dawns upon us, self-concern is seen to be a
> drifting alien body, untethered from its moorings, that
> forms no part of who we really are. It is dislodged from
> its position as the seemingly indestructible centre of
> motivation.[85]

In practising Buddhist ethics, which are founded upon empathy, we come to gradually understand that others are as we are. Others too have hopes and fears, joys and sorrows, come into this world alone, and die alone. The more we realize this on a gut level, the less possible it is to desire freedom and happiness for ourselves alone. And this is true even if we're practising in deepest solitude. Mahayana Buddhism, which was partly a reaction to overscholasticism and sought to re-emphasize the kind of compassionate activity of which the Buddha was the prime exemplar, stressed the Bodhicitta. The Bodhicitta is the deep and heartfelt desire for Enlightenment, not just for oneself alone, but for all sentient beings. When the Bodhicitta truly arises in our heart and consciousness, we are transformed, because in truly desiring the welfare of others as we do our own, we are going beyond self-concern and ego. We are realizing, as opposed to understanding theoretically, our relatedness. Santideva, the

famous eleventh-century Mahayana Buddhist, sought to inspire
the rising of the Bodhicitta in the hearts of practitioners in verses
like these:

> We love our hands and other limbs, as members of
> the body; then why not love other living beings as
> members of the Universe? By constant use man comes
> to imagine that his body, which has no self-being, is a
> 'self': why then should he not conceive his 'self' to lie in
> his fellows also?[86]

Such empathy is what spiritual community or Sangha is
trying to generate. In committing ourselves to Sangha, we are
attempting to realize the indivisibility of all beings. And because
the Bodhicitta is a recognition of relatedness, it is not surprising
that Sangharakshita believes such profound empathy is most
likely to arise within a community:

> [The Bodhicitta] is more likely to arise in the case
> of a number of people working hard together, and
> stimulating and sparking one another off, rather
> than in the solitary individual, in whose case it may
> tend to be more like an individual experience in the
> narrower sense. At the same time it is not a 'collective'
> thing in the sense of a product of mass psychology.
> We don't really have a word for it. It's more a
> matter of fellowship, or a manifestation of spiritual
> communion.[87]

Genius seems to stand alone. William Shakespeare, for example,
seems to be a towering and unique talent. But Shakespeare was
part of the extraordinary blossoming of artists, writers, poets,
and statesmen that took place during the Elizabethan age and

also produced Marlowe, Sidney, Jonson, and Raleigh. One has a sense that these men drew from one another, inspired one another, were inspired by their queen, and flourished in a spirit of positive competitiveness. The same sense of mutual inspiration and positive competitiveness operates within an effective spiritual community.

Sangharakshita has described the spiritual community as 'a coincidence of wills', a collection of men and women who are working to realize a shared vision. Subjugating one's ego in this way is different from submerging one's character or subscribing to some dull uniformity. Reading the early Buddhist scriptures, we have a sense that the Buddha's main disciples were uniformly inspired but not of a uniform character. Two of these disciples, the great friends Moggallana and Sariputta, could hardly have been more different. Moggallana was a visionary with a capacity to experience the psychic, and Sariputta a scholar who didn't seem to have had many psychic experiences at all!

One of my own experiences of spiritual community at its best took place during a meeting with quite a few other members of the Triratna Buddhist Order. There were about twenty of us present during the meeting and we were discussing the arrangements for the funeral of a friend. Everyone seemed to bring their own individual perspective to bear on the discussion, while allowing their views to be tempered by others. Nobody was pressing their own views in an egotistical way at all and, by the end of the meeting, we had come to an agreement and a synthesis which seemed hugely satisfying. We'd done the best for our friend and something had emerged in that meeting that had felt quite magical. The metaphor of an orchestra might be a useful one in considering occasions like this, when the Sangha is working effectively. In the orchestra there are many different musical instruments, each with its own unique sound, but each instrument contributes to the whole. And it is the music of the orchestra that matters in the end. I like the orchestra metaphor because it's a fluid, dynamic one. It also evokes harmony and unity, which, of course, are the aims of spiritual community.

I've spent this whole chapter talking about relatedness and spiritual community to emphasize that, for a Buddhist, practice in solitude is always done in the context of a heartfelt desire not just for one's own welfare, but for the welfare of all beings. In the previous chapter I said that solitude should be relished for its own sake, and not for what one can squeeze out of it, but, necessarily, if we're practising effectively in a Buddhist context, we will be challenged to become more outward-looking – to love more deeply. In researching this book, it is this altruistic sense that I've found lacking in some (although certainly not all) of the books I've read on solitude. An individualistic quest where one's solitude is guarded fiercely with little regard for others is not the Buddhist way.

In this book we've seen that time spent in solitude, and the capacity to be alone, is very much part of the Buddhist path and, if practised effectively, can generate the empathy and desire for renunciation that can take us beyond the ego. In this process, one of the things we may find we have to renounce is our solitary individualism. We may have spent the first period of our spiritual life struggling to separate ourselves from unhelpful conditioning, creating for ourselves a new set of values to supplant some of the beliefs and assumptions we grew up with, beliefs that may have invited conformity and passive acceptance. In the process, we may have become rather attached to these new ideas of ours, feel relatively self-sufficient and suspicious of any organized system of beliefs whatsoever. But, in order to progress, there will come a time when we'll need to swallow our pride and put our experience into some kind of tried and tested context; when we will need to find like-minded individuals and kindred spirits; when we'll need to accept the hands of the wise who have come before us. We may, for example, have strong meditation experiences, which we might not be able to understand or might misinterpret, without the help of some more traditional perspective.

On my very first solitary retreat I found myself at a dead end. I'd been having, for want of a better phrase, 'spiritual experiences', and had interpreted these in my own particular, and eccentric, way. But I was beginning to realize that my interpretation of these experiences was leading me into areas of confusion, and worse. I'd forged my own kind of religion but was beginning to realize how inadequate and dangerous my 'religion' really was. I needed a context. One night I had a dream. A Buddhist I'd met on a recent retreat was sitting beside me in his scarlet tunic. He was a funny, kind, wild, and genuinely spiritual person, and I admired him very much. Gently he took my hand. 'Join the Sangha', he grinned. I felt a strange mixture of emotions when he said this – relief, understanding, but also a kind of grief. It is sometimes very difficult to surrender the belief that you can go it alone. But surrendering that belief was the beginning, for me, of the journey from isolation and loneliness.

6

Conclusion

Message in a Bottle

I am now worth 800 pounds, but shall never be so happy, as when I was not worth a Farthing.[88]

Alexander Selkirk, the inspiration
for Robinson Crusoe.

Desert Island Discs is a famous and long-running British radio programme in which a celebrity is invited to choose the eight favourite records, the favourite book, and one luxury item they would take with them were they to go to a desert island. Perhaps it's time now for you to make your own choices . . . Because your ship has just vanished over the horizon. You're entirely alone on your desert island. You wade back through the shallows to the shore. Next to the supplies you've been left sits a deckchair, and next to the deckchair, a table, upon which stands an old gramophone. Beside the gramophone sit your eight favourite records. (What are they and which will you play first?) Also on the table lies your favourite book (what is it?), as well as one Buddhist book (and what's that?). Next to the gramophone table there sits a crate, and in the crate is your luxury item. (What is it?) On top of the crate there is a pen and a corked bottle with a note inside it. You uncork the bottle and read the note. It says:

Please specify the duration of your stay. That is, when do you wish to be rescued? Please also specify the name of the first person you wish to meet on your return home.

You fill in the note. (What do you write?) Then you replace the note, cork the bottle, and throw it into the sea. Then you sit down on the deckchair, and . . .

Appendix

Nettle Soup

It is said that Milarepa survived on a diet of nettle soup. Here a contemporary Buddhist chef, Vimalabandhu, offers advice on how to cook Milarepa's favourite – albeit only – dish:

> Milarepa had only an earthen bowl, fire, and nettles. So he had no choice but to cook the nettles in water and eat them. For us today – we softies – our solitary facilities may have pots and pans, cooking oil, onions, potatoes or flour, salt and some spices or herbs. Therefore we can do some reflection and experimentation to find 'the truth' of cooking. We can ask ourselves: what kind of food do we want to make with the nettles and other ingredients available?
>
> A preliminary caution: nettles sting, including their young leaves. One needs to wear gloves or other protection to pick them and once collected scald them with boiling water to eliminate the sting.
>
> Then you can try treating young nettles as spinach and prepare a substitute of a spinach dish you know. Or, particularly if onions and potatoes are available, try to make a nettle and potato soup in the way of leek and potato soup. Evaluate your culinary experiment and

make adjustments for a more satisfactory result – for example, by adding or reducing herbs and spices or other ingredients and by changing the cooking time, the heat, and so on. And of course you can do this with any other edible ingredient.

Notes

1 William Cowper, 'The Solitude of Alexander Selkirk', available from http://www.bartleby.com/106/160.html.
2 Quoted in an appendix to Daniel Defoe, *Robinson Crusoe*, Penguin Classics, London 1965, p.310.
3 *Ekavihariya: dwelling alone*, translated from the Pali by Thanissaro Bhikkhu, available from the Access to Insight website at http://www.accesstoinsight.org/tipitaka/kn/thag/thag.10.02.than.html (PTS: Thag. 537–46).
4 Emily Dickinson, 'A choice of Emily Dickinson's verse', in *Emily Dickinson: poems*, selected by Ted Hughes, Faber, London 1968, pp.46–7.
5 Charles Chaplin, *My Autobiography*, Penguin Modern Classics, London 2003, p.180.
6 Sangharakshita, *The Yogi's Joy*, Windhorse Publications, Birmingham 2006, p.15.
7 Richard Sennett, quoted in *Hopper*, ed. Ivo Kranzfelder, Taschen, London 2006, pp.150–1.
8 R.D. Laing, *The Divided Self*, Penguin, London 1982, p.205.
9 *Duhkha* (Sanskrit) or *dukkha* (Pali) is usually translated as 'pain', 'suffering', or 'unsatisfactoriness'.
10 Trevor Ling, *The Buddha*, Temple Smith, London 1985, p.62.

11 Introduction to *Mitrata*, a bimonthly magazine for Mitras (lit. friends) affiliated to the (then) Western Buddhist Order, now the Triratna Buddhist Order.

12 Advert on the Fascination perfumery website, http://www. fascination-perfumery.co.uk.

13 *They Shoot Horses, Don't They?*, directed by Sydney Pollack, Palomar films, 1969.

14 Horace McCoy, *They Shoot Horses, Don't They?*, Serpent's Tail, London 1995, p.76.

15 *The Hundred Thousand Songs of Milarepa*, translated by Garma C.C. Chang, 2 vols, Shambala, Boston 1962, vol.1, p.63.

16 Sangharakshita, *Mind Reactive and Creative*, Windhorse Publications, Birmingham 1989, p.12.

17 Quoted in Jack Kornfield, *The Wise Heart*, Rider, London 2008, p.337.

18 Blaise Pascal, *Thoughts*, Penguin Classics, London 1995, Thought 139.

19 Sangharakshita, *The Yogi's Joy*, pp.15–16.

20 Sangharakshita, *Mind Reactive and Creative*, p.12.

21 *Maha-Parinibanna Sutta: last days of the Buddha*, translated from the Pali by Sister Vajira and Francis Story, part 2 verse 33, available from the Access to Insight website at http://www. accesstoinsight.org/tipitaka/dn/dn.16.1-6.vaji.html (PTS: D.ii.72).

22 Quoted in Kornfield, *The Wise Heart*, p.131.

23 Anthony de Mello, *Awareness*, Fount, London 1997, p.163.

24 Anthony Storr, *Solitude*, Flamingo, London 1989, p.xiv.

25 Storr, *Solitude*, p.xiv.

26 Poem included in Roger Housden, *Ten Poems to Change Your Life*, Hodder, London 2003, p.95.

27 Emerson, 'Self-Reliance', in *Complete Prose Works*, Ward, Lock and Co., n.p., n.d., p.15.

28 Philip Larkin, 'Best Society', in *Collected Poems*, Faber, London 2001, pp.56–7.

29 Emerson, 'Self-Reliance', p.17.

30 Franz Kafka, from *Betrachtungen über Sünde, Leid, Hoffnung und den wahren Weg* (translated as *Reflections on Sin, Suffering, Hope and the True Way*), published after Kafka's death in *Beim Bau der chinesischen Mauer* (translated as *The Great Wall of China: Stories and Reflections*). This statement is found at the end of Kafka's last aphorism, number 109.

31 Sangharakshita, *The Yogi's Joy*, p.139.

32 Quoted in *Acts of Light: poems by Emily Dickinson*, ed. Jane Langton, Bulfinch Press, Boston 1980, p.47.

33 Quoted in *Acts of Light*, p.111.

34 Quoted in *Acts of Light*, p.16.

35 Roger Lewis, *The Life and Death of Peter Sellers*, London, Arrow Books, 1995, p.xxv.

36 Stephen Batchelor, *Alone with Others*, Grove Press, New York 1983, pp.27–8.

37 Mello, *Awareness*, p.165.

38 Sangharakshita, *The Yogi's Joy*, p.154.

39 Vicki Mackenzie, *Cave in the Snow*, Bloomsbury, London 1998, p.171.

40 Both quotes from Natalie Goldberg, *Wild Mind*, Rider, London 1991, p.xiii.

41 *The Life of Milarepa*, translated by Lonsang P. Lhalungpa, Granada, London 1979, p.102.

42 Sangharakshita, *The Yogi's Joy*, p.58.

43 Henry David Thoreau, *Walden; or, Life in the Woods*, Dover Publications, New York 1995, p.59.

44 Goldberg, *Wild Mind*, p.xiii.

45 William Shakespeare, *As You Like It*, act 2, scene 1, lines 16–17, in *The Complete Works*, Oxford University Press, Oxford 1998, p.634.

46 Gerald Manley Hopkins, *Poems and Prose*, Penguin, London 1971, p.61.

47 William Wordsworth, 'Lines Composed a Few Miles above Tintern Abbey', lines 25–9, in *The Works of William Wordsworth*, Wordsworth Poetry Library, Ware 1994, p.206.

48 Wordsworth, 'Tintern Abbey', p.207.

49 Wordsworth, 'Tintern Abbey', p.206.

50 S.T. Coleridge, *Lyrical Ballads*, Methuen, London 1975, pp.19–20.

51 Edmund Burke, quoted in *The Oxford Book of the Sea*, ed. Jonathan Raban, Oxford University Press, Oxford 1993, p.9.

52 Sangharakshita, *The Taste of Freedom*, Windhorse Publications, Birmingham 1997, pp.19–20.

53 Storr, *Solitude*, p.32.

54 Thoreau, *Walden*, p.60.

55 Thoreau, *Walden*, p.61.

56 Sara Maitland, *A Book of Silence*, Granta Books, London 2008, p.221.

57 Sangharakshita, *The Taste of Freedom*, p.20.

58 Emerson, 'Self-Reliance', p.17.

59 Anthony de Mello, *The Way to Love*, Doubleday, New York 1995, p.10.

60 William Shakespeare, *Hamlet*, act 3, scene 1, lines 81–2, in *The Complete Works*, p.670.

61 Kamala Tiyavanich, *Forest Recollections*, University of Hawaii Press, Hawaii 1997, p.100.

62 Tiyavanich, *Forest Recollections*, p.105.

63 Sangharakshita, *The Yogi's Joy*, p.56.

64 *Bhaya-bherava sutta: fear and terror*, translated from the Pali by Thanissaro Bhikkhu, available from the Access to Insight website at http://www.accesstoinsight.org/tipitaka/mn/mn.004.than.html (PTS: M.i.16).

65 Quoted by Peter Nichols, *A Voyage for Madmen*, Profile Books, London 2002, p.272.

Appendix

66 Nichols, *A Voyage for Madmen*.

67 Nichols, *A Voyage for Madmen*, p.89.

68 Mackenzie, *Cave in the Snow*, p.4.

69 *The Meghiya sutta: about Meghiya*, translated from the Pali by Thanissaro Bhikkhu, available from the Access to Insight website at http://www.accesstoinsight.org/tipitaka/kn/ud/ud.4.01.than.html (PTS: Ud. 34).

70 Jon Krakauer, *Into the Wild*, Anchor Press, New York 1996, p.159.

71 Krakauer, *Into the Wild*, p.163.

72 Krakauer, *Into the Wild*, p.187.

73 Krakauer, *Into the Wild*, p.189.

74 Krakauer, *Into the Wild*, p.189.

75 William Blake, 'Jerusalem', in *Complete Writings*, Oxford University Press, Oxford 1992, p.622.

76 Sangharakshita, *The Yogi's Joy*, p.106.

77 Alan Bennett, *The History Boys*, Faber, London 2006, p.107.

78 Bennett, *The History Boys*, p.61.

79 Defoe, *Robinson Crusoe*, p.130.

80 Sangharakshita, *The Yogi's Joy*, p.16.

81 Sam Keen, *Fire in the Belly: on being a man*, Piatkus, London 1992, p.190.

82 Storr, *Solitude*, p.xiv.

83 Ling, *The Buddha*, p.124.

84 Ling, *The Buddha*, p.127, emphasis added.

85 Batchelor, *Alone with Others*, p.84.

86 Santideva quoted by Sangharakshita in *The Ten Pillars of Buddhism*, Windhorse Publications, Cambridge 2010, p.71.

87 Subhuti, *Sangharakshita*, Windhorse Publications, Birmingham 1994, p.128.

88 Quoted in an appendix to Defoe, *Robinson Crusoe*, p.310.

Recommended Reading

My main inspiration for this book was Sangharakshita's *The Yogi's Joy*, Windhorse Publications, Birmingham 2006. Here are some other books that I drew upon and recommend:

Batchelor, Stephen, *Alone with Others*, Grove Press, New York 1983.

Dickinson, Emily, *Acts of Light: poems by Emily Dickinson*, ed. Jane Langton, Bulfinch Press, Boston 1980.

—, *Emily Dickinson: poems*, selected by Ted Hughes, Faber, London 1968.

The Hundred Thousand Songs of Milarepa, translated by Garma C.C. Chang, 2 vols, Shambala, Boston 1962.

Krakauer, Jon, *Into the Wild*, Anchor Press, New York 1996.

Ling, Trevor, *The Buddha*, Temple Smith, London 1985.

Mackenzie, Vicki, *Cave in the Snow*, Bloomsbury, London 1998.

Maitland, Sara, *A Book of Silence*, Granta Books, London 2008.

Mello, Anthony de, *Awareness*, Fount, London 1997.

Nichols, Peter, *A Voyage for Madmen*, Profile Books, London 2002.

Sangharakshita, *Mind Reactive and Creative*, Windhorse Publications, Birmingham 1989.

—, *The Taste of Freedom*, Windhorse Publications, Birmingham 1997.

Solitude and Loneliness

Storr, Anthony, *Solitude*, Flamingo, London 1989.
Tiyavanich, Kamala, *Forest Recollections*, University of Hawaii Press, Hawaii 1997.

I would also like to recommend the Access to Insight website, available at www.accesstoinsight.org, and the Free Buddhist Audio website, available at www.freebuddhistaudio.com.

WINDHORSE PUBLICATIONS

Windhorse Publications is a Buddhist charitable company based in the UK. We place great emphasis on producing books of high quality that are accessible and relevant to those interested in Buddhism at whatever level. We are the main publisher of the works of Sangharakshita, the founder of the Triratna Buddhist Order and Community. Our books draw on the whole range of the Buddhist tradition, including translations of traditional texts, commentaries, books that make links with contemporary culture and ways of life, biographies of Buddhists, and works on meditation.

As a not-for-profit enterprise, we ensure that all surplus income is invested in new books and improved production methods, to better communicate Buddhism in the 21st Century. We welcome donations to help us continue our work - to find out more, go to www.windhorsepublications.com.

The Windhorse is a mythical animal that flies over the earth carrying on its back three precious jewels, bringing these invaluable gifts to all humanity: the Buddha (the 'awakened one') his teaching, and the community of all his followers.

Windhorse Publications
169 Mill Road
Cambridge CB1 3AN
UK
info@windhorsepublications.com

Perseus Distribution
1094 Flex Drive
Jackson TN 38301
USA

Windhorse Books
PO Box 574
Newtown NSW 2042
Australia

THE TRIRATNA BUDDHIST COMMUNITY

Windhorse Publications is a part of the Triratna Buddhist Community, which has more than sixty centres on five continents. Through these centres, members of the Triratna Buddhist Order offer classes in meditation and Buddhism, from an introductory to deeper levels of commitment. Bodywork classes such as yoga, Tai chi, and massage are also taught at many Triratna centres. Members of the Triratna community run retreat centres around the world, and the Karuna Trust, a UK fundraising charity that supports social welfare projects in the slums and villages of South Asia.

Many Triratna centres have residential spiritual communities and ethical Right Livelihood businesses associated with them. Arts activities are encouraged too, as is the development of strong bonds of friendship between people who share the same ideals. In this way Triratna is developing a unique approach to Buddhism, not simply as a set of techniques, but as a creatively directed way of life for people living in the modern world.

If you would like more information about Triratna please visit www.thebuddhistcentre.com or write to:

London Buddhist Centre
51 Roman Road
London E2 0HU
UK

Aryaloka
14 Heartwood Circle
Newmarket NH 03857
USA

Sydney Buddhist Centre
24 Enmore Road
Sydney NSW 2042
Australia

Also from Windhorse Publications

A Buddhist View series

Meditating: A Buddhist View
by Jinananda

Meditation is a household word, everyone has their idea of what it is, but does this mean that it is more misunderstood than understood? Here Jinananda, an experienced meditation teacher, gives us the Buddhist perspective. He shows us that – far from being a safe, patching-up, therapeutic tool – meditation is a radical, transformative, waking-up practice.

Buddhist meditation is about being true to your experience, and this means getting behind the idea of what is going on, behind the label, to the ungraspable experience of this moment. Jinananda shows you how to start doing this, how to sit comfortably for meditation, and how to do two meditation practices that develop clarity, peace of mind and positive emotions.

ISBN 9781 9073140 6 3
£8.99 / $13.95 / €10.95
160 pages

Finding the Mind: A Buddhist View
by Robin Cooper

'Here am I, in this body I call my own, among millions that are mysteriously other. What's going on?' You may have asked this, or something like it, at some point in your life. How can you find the answer?

Buddhism points to your own mind as a way to understand and transform your experience. But, as Robin Cooper explains, it takes an exploratory approach, it asks you to seek: it is not a revelation of religious truths. The Buddha saw that we are all in a tough predicament. We are constantly anxious about what we lack and what we may lose, and in chasing security we easily cause pain to others. But the Buddha did not offer to save us through faith in his truth. Instead, he asked us to explore. Be aware, probe the edges of your awareness, investigate, and find your mind.

ISBN 9781 9073140 3 2
£8.99 / $13.95 / € 10.95
160 pages

Meaning in Life: A Buddhist View
by Sarvananda

How can we bring more sense of significance into our lives? What meaning does life have in the face of suffering or death? Do we have a 'why' to live for?

Sarvananda draws a parallel between the Buddha's quest and our own search for meaning in the modern world. Using references from the 20th century, he covers many of the ways in which we seek meaning, citing writers and thinkers such as Akira Kurosawa, Wordsworth and Woody Allen. In so doing he moves from individual understanding to the principles of Buddhist teaching and demonstrates in a calm, friendly way how to apply the teachings practically, before finally taking the reader to a deeper reality.

A concise, witty exploration of what truly matters.

ISBN 9781 899579 87 7
£7.99 / $13.95 / €9.95
144 pages

Vegetarianism: A Buddhist View
by Bodhipaksa

How does what we eat affect us and our world? Is there a connection between vegetarianism and living a spiritual life? Doesn't HH the Dalai Lama eat meat?

A trained vet, respected teacher and happy vegan, Bodhipaksa answers all of these questions and more. Tackling issues such as genetically modified vegetables and modern ways of producing food he dispels widespread myths and reflects upon the diets dominant in the contemporary West. In comparison, he considers the diets of wandering monks in Ancient India and the diet of the Buddha himself.

By considering why people eat meat and relating this to Buddhist ethics he explores habits and the possibility of change. He takes a positive view of the benefits of vegetarianism, and shows practically, how to maintain a healthy and balanced vegan or vegetarian lifestyle.

This exploration shows how a meat-free life can not only lighten the body but also the soul.

ISBN 9781 899579 96 9
£7.99 / $13.95 / €9.95
104 pages

Buddhism: Tools for Living Your Life
By Vajragupta

In this guide for all those seeking a meaningful spiritual path,
Vajragupta provides clear explanations of the main Buddhist teachings,
as well as a variety of exercises designed to help readers develop or
deepen their practice.

*Appealing, readable, and practical, blending accessible teachings, practices, and
personal stories . . . as directly relevant to modern life as it is comprehensive
and rigorous.* – Tricycle: The Buddhist Review, 2007

*I'm very pleased that someone has finally written this book! At last, a real
'toolkit' for living a Buddhist life, his practical suggestions are hard to resist!* –
Saddhanandi, Chair of Taraloka Retreat Centre

ISBN 9781 899579 74 7
£10.99 / $16.95 / €16.95
192 pages

A Path for Parents
by Sara Burns

A Path for Parents is for anyone interested in spiritual life within the
context of parenting. Sara Burns, mother and Buddhist practitioner,
draws on her own experience to deliver a refreshingly honest and
accessible account of how parents can grow spiritually among their
everyday experiences of life with children.

ISBN 9781 899579 70 9
£11.99 / $17.95 / €17.95
176 pages

Wildmind: A Step-by-Step Guide to Meditation
by Bodhipaksa

From how to build your own stool to how a raisin can help you meditate, this illustrated guide explains everything you need to know to start or strengthen your meditation practice. This best-seller is in a new handy format and features brand new illustrations.

Of great help to people interested in meditation and an inspiring reminder to those on the path. – Joseph Goldstein, cofounder of the Insight Meditation Society and author of *One Dharma: The Emerging Western Buddhism*

Bodhipaksa has written a beautiful and very accessible introduction to meditation. He guides us through all the basics of mindfulness and also loving-kindness meditations with the voice of a wise, kind, and patient friend. – Dr. Lorne Ladner, author of *The Lost Art of Compassion*

ISBN 9781 899579 91 4
£9.99 / $16.95 / €11.95
240 pages